The 2D Games Journey

A Progressive Study of 2D Games and Essential Algorithms in Flash ActionScript 3.0

Dana Vrajitoru

Dana Vrajitoru

ISBN: 1492269573
ISBN-13: 978-1492269571

Contents

1. Introduction

This book represents an introduction to 2D games using Flash ActionScript 3.0 as a platform. It approaches the field in a progressive way, classifying games in categories based on essential features and difficulty. It combines discussions on practical games and implementation details with topics pertaining to games theory. Our intention is to familiarize the reader with a set of games with enough variety to provide a solid background for approaching any other 2D game with ease.

Games programming is a popular topic among computer science majors. Part of the interest comes form the fact that the gaming industry is one of the most successful computing branches. Part of it stems from the fact that people who enjoy playing games would like a chance to create their own. This topic offers interesting challenges and rewards to the programmer and it a solid stepping stone for beginner coders. It gives them an opportunity to hone their skills and learn more about the craft.

This book is designed with two audiences in mind. First, for independent programmers with at least a modest coding background who wish to start writing games. Second, for college teachers in a computer science degree who offer one course in games programming as part of their electives and their students. It is meant as a first introduction to the field and does not assume prior experience.

The chosen language is ActionScript 3.0, the basis for Flash applications. We have chosen it because online games, and Flash games in particular, currently represent one of the most popular platforms for games and the easiest way for a programmer to reach an audience. The language is easy to learn for anyone with a C, C++, or Java background. It is object-oriented and offers many utilities for integrating multimedia components in an application. Thus, it is an ideal language to start in this field.

The book is not designed to be a thorough introduction to ActionScript programming, but rather uses it as a tool for discussing games. However, we also do not expect prior knowledge of the language, but only general familiarity with object-oriented programming. We'll provide a brief introduction to it and hope that through the coding tutorials provided in the subsequent chapters, the reader will acquire a solid ActionScript foundation. We also hope that the book will encourage the reader to further explore aspects of the language not covered here by seeking additional materials.

The book is structured in such a way as to introduce the reader progressively to 2D games. We start with a chapter containing elements of game theory and design. A second chapter discusses general purpose implementation details applying to many games. Next, we classify the games based on complexity and provide a tutorial containing detailed instructions to write a game from each category. One chapter is dedicated to games that do not require animation, called reactive games, and the next one to animated games. We hope that by the end of the book, we have introduced the reader to a good number of games with a variety of structures such that he or she will be able to write their own game successfully.

1.1. 2D Arcade Games

The name of "arcade" games comes from the coin-operated machines that were popular in the early 70s and beyond. Historically, these machines can be considered the first easily accessible and popular medium for digital games. The limits of the available technology at the time pushed games writers to find ingenious ways to create appealing and addictive game content. Many of the games that emerged from those early years are still crowd favorites and considered among the best ever invented. New versions or emulations of those games can be found on various platforms, including online.

These games feature a world often composed of a finite number of cells of size larger than a pixel. We can call such a world "discrete". The critters are iconic characters, drawn on small bitmaps in a limited number of colors. For example, colors represented on 8 bits result in a palette of 256 colors, such as the set of "system colors". This representation is also the origin of the name of "8-bit pixel art". Many of these games present multiple levels of rapidly increasing difficulty. They feature simple animation techniques, such as circular textures. Their storyline is usually limited, although some have made special efforts in this direction. The learning curve is generally easy, as the game mechanisms are learned while focusing mostly on the player's skills. They rely either on speed of reaction or on logical puzzle solving.

ActionScript and Flash technology are bringing a new life to these classic games, making them available to play online. Seasoned players are finding new versions of the games they love and new players are being introduced to them.

The classic setting of the game is a 2D table or arena. It is characterized by a small number of cells of relatively large size, comprising several pixels each, and with integer coordinates. We can call this a discrete world, as opposed to a continuous world made of real coordinates.

In many implementations the cells of the table represent individual objects and contain them entirely. Their movement is then accomplished by skipping from one cell to the next. In more recent games, though, objects can expand over one or more cells and they can cross over cell boundaries during the process of movement, which makes it look continuous.

The game is composed of several entities, objects or characters, interacting with each other and the player. They are oftentimes called sprites. Some of them are only decorative while others have independent movement and even behavior.

The game has a goal and a score. The game can sometimes be won, or simply played until it is lost. Thus, in a game of PacMan, the player can finish each available level, thus winning the game. In a game of Tetris, however, the game continues until it is lost, and challenge consists in achieving a high score and lasting for a long time in the game.

1.2. ActionScript 3.0

ActionScript is an object oriented programming language designed to support interactive multimedia content on web pages. It was originally created by Macromedia in 1996 along with Flash. In its current version 3.0, it is owned by Adobe and is an open source language. Version 2.0, dating from 2004, introduced user-defined classes stored in external files, which greatly contributed to a better organization and structuring of the code. Version 3.0, launched in 2006, is a more standardized language and runs much faster than the previous code on a completely rewritten virtual machine. It is now a fully object-oriented language.

ActionScript is quite similar in syntax to JavaScript, Java, and C++. It is in fact considered as part of the JavaScript family. Some call it strictly typed because methods and operations must be applied to data of the right type. Other sources call it weakly or loosely typed because types are associated with the objects and values and not with variables, parameters, and values returned from functions. Thus, even if a variable is initially assigned an integer value, it can be assigned a real value later in the execution stream.

An ActionScript application requires a Flash player plug-in or application to run. The code is compiled as a file with the extension **.swf** that can be run on its own or embedded in a web page. The programs are called apps or movies, and they are heavily event-driven. The ActionScript code resides in action panels that can be added to Flash frames, button, or movie clips, or in external files. Typically, each file contains one class and bears the class name with the extension **.as**,. The action panels are attached to Frames, Buttons, or Movie Clips. The code in a panel attached to an entity or clip controls its behavior.

A flash project has the extension **.fla** and contains the resources and the code defining an application. The visible part of the program where everything is displayed is called the *stage*. One can find in the project objects created in the stage, resources imported to the stage, and code that was added directly to panels. It is organized in frames and scenes composing a timeline.

As mentioned above, *variables* do not need types when they are declared, but a type can be specified. Flash can suggest appropriate methods for that particular data type if one is provided. Variables are declared with the keyword **var** followed by the name of the variable. An optional colon followed by a type can specify a type for the variable. The declaration can also assign an initial value to the variable. Here is an example of such a declaration:

```
var name:String = "John";
```

Variables are local to the scope in which they are declared. If one is declared inside a function body, then it is local to the function. Variables declared in an action panel are global but only within the code in that action panel.

Let us now examine the syntax of *control structures* such as conditionals and loops. The familiar curly braces from C++ have the same meaning here: to group instructions in a block. They are not mandatory in the context of a conditional or a loop, but recommended for a better understanding of the code. They also help the ActionScript editor with syntax checking.

Conditionals have the same syntax as in C++ and JavaScript, as seen in the example below. The **else** part is optional, just like in any other language.

```
if (x == "food")
{
    Eat(x);
}
else
{
    dontEat(x);
}
```

There are two types of *loops* following the C++ structure: the `for` loop and the `while` loop. The following `for` loop below executes the conditional exactly 7 times.

```
for (i = 0; i<7; i++)
    if (found == false)
        gameover = false;
```

The following `while` loop calls the function "`play`" for as long as the condition "not game over" is true.

```
while (!gameover)
{
    play();
}
```

Functions are a vital part of any language. In ActionScript the parameters don't need specific types, but a type can be provided the same way as for variables. The definition must start with the keyword `function` followed by the function name. In the example below, we declare the function called `displayArea`, with two parameters, printing a debugging message, and then returning the product of the two parameters.

```
function displayArea (width, height)
{
    trace(width * height);
    return width*height;
}
```

The type of the returned value can also be specified, just like for parameters. Here is another version of the header of the function above with types provided both for the parameters and for the returned value:

```
function displayArea (width :int,
                      height :int):int
```

Functions are called with a syntax similar to C++:

```
displayArea(10, 20);
```

Most ActionScript programs need to react to *events*. Here is an example of code that could be found in the action panel of a button:

```
on (release)
{
    if (words._visible == true)
    {
        setProperty(words, _visible, false);
    }
    else
    {
        setProperty(words, _visible, true);
    }
}
```

Here **words** is a reference to an object (image) to be displayed on the web page. It has a property that allows it to be visible or not. **release** is an event generated by the release of the mouse button. **on (event)** is a special syntax that defines behavior related to an event.

In ActionScript 3.0, most of the events are added to the objects they relate to with a call to the function addEventListener, described generically as

```
object.addEventListener(event, function);
```

This function call will connect the object with the event provided as parameter. When the event occurs, the function specified as the second parameter is called. For this reason, we're referring to it as a *callback* function.

ActionScript 3.0 has an extensive library of *classes* for all kind of purposes. It also allows the programmers to define their own classes in external files and import them into a Flash project. This increases the reusability of the code as compared to previous versions.

The following code shows some examples of useful classes. The class **Sprite** defines objects that can be displayed on the stage at any given position. The class **BitmapData** can hold an image loaded as a resource in the project. The class **Timer** provides a tool allowing for a function to be called at regular intervals. As seen below, the operator **new** allows for objects of each of these classes to be created using a constructor with or without parameters. The function **addEventListener** connects the timer event, generated at regular intervals, to the function **scrollLayers** to be called when the event occurs.

```
var skySprite:Sprite = new Sprite();
var tile:BitmapData = new SkyBg(550, 700);
skySprite.graphics.drawRect(0, 0, tile.width,
                            tile.height);
var scroll_timer:Timer = new Timer(5);
scroll_timer.addEventListener(TimerEvent.TIMER,
                            scrollLayers);
scroll_timer.start();
```

Let's take a look at the *user-defined classes*. The code for a class must be placed in a file by the same name as the class and with extension **.as**. In the file, the class must be in a **package** named after the subdirectory the class is in, or without a name if the class is in the same directory as the project.

As one can find from any textbook on object-oriented

languages, classes are data structures containing data fields, or attributes, and functions called class methods. In ActionScript 3.0, attributes are simply variables declared inside the class. Class methods are functions defined inside the class. They can both be declared **public**, but by default they are **internal**, which is equivalent to **private** if the class is not part of a named package.

A class should have a *constructor*, which is a function with the same name as the class and called to create new objects of this class. Only one constructor is allowed, unlike in other languages such as C++. However, the parameters can have optional values specified with the syntax **par = val**.

For example, let's define a class called **Rectangle**, derived from the class **Sprite**, with attributes **width** and **height**. We will need to import the package containing the class **Sprite**. We would have a constructor for it with two parameters, both having default values, and a class method called **draw**, with no parameters. Then the class file **Rectangle.as** would have the following content:

```
package
{
    import flash.display.Sprite;

    // Class declaration
    class Rectangle: public Sprite
    {
        var width, height; // attributes

        // Constructor
        public function Rectangle(w = 1, h = 1)
        {
            width = w;
            height = h;
        }
```

```
    // A class method
    public function draw()
    {
        . . .
    }
}
}
```

Then to create an object of the class **Rectangle**, we would first have to import the module **Rectangle** the same way we imported the **Sprite** package, then we can use the syntax

```
var r = new Rectangle(10, 20);
```

Once we have an object, we can call a class method with the dot syntax, in the manner of C++:

```
r.draw();
```

This brief introduction is by no means exhaustive and is only designed to allow the reader to understand the syntax of the code discussed in further chapters. The most reliable and up to date documentation on this language is the Adobe web site (Adobe, 2013).

Dana Vrajitoru

2. Elements of Game Design

In this chapter we are going to discuss some organizational ideas related to games, to what they are, and how they are structured. For the readers with more interest in the subject, (Salem & Zimmerman, 2004) is a good reference and contains longer discussion on similar topics. For the casual game programmer who is not that interested in the theory of games, we hope that this chapter will provide enough of a foundation to get started.

Many authors and books offer definitions of what a game is. Even though the answer to this question may seem obvious to anyone who has ever played a game, and it comes so natural to young children, as game designers, we should start by defining the object of our pursuit precisely.

A clever definition of a game was given by Bernard Suits in (Suits, 1990): "Playing a game is the voluntary effort to overcome unnecessary obstacles."

To summarize many such definitions from a variety of sources, we can see the game as:

- A *system* - a game is a system, or a set of interacting elements.
- *Players* – a game requires one or more voluntary participants. The voluntary aspect is important, although exceptions can be found in the literature or even in real life.
- *Goal* – every game involves achieving a goal. In some cases the goal is quantifiable, other times not.
- *Rules* – they create the structure defining how the game is played, what the players are allowed to do, what they are

required to do, and what they are forbidden to do. The rules define the context for achieving the goal of the game.

- *Artificial* – games represent an environment created for the sole purpose of the game. While the players are engaged in the act of playing, they are granted an exclusive existence inside the world of the game.
- *Conflict* – a game involves one form or another of contest: either between players, or between the players and the environment. It can be implicit or explicit. It is the nature of the game to offer obstacles towards the achievement of the goal.

2.1 Digital Games

Digital games follow the general rules that apply to material games, but they also present special features that set them apart from them. These features make the game play more dramatic and appealing, but they also represent an additional challenge for the programmers.

In terms of *interactivity*, digital games offer immediate but narrow interaction. It is limited to the available input, such as mouse, keyboard, controller, and to the available output, such as screen and speakers. More importantly, it is limited to what the programmer has made available. What the player expects of these games in terms of interaction is real-time response. For this reason, it is important that efficient algorithms are implemented for all the aspects of the game requiring expensive calculations, such as the graphics display and collision detection.

As any other software program, digital games perform a good deal of *information manipulation*. They need to store and use data about the game elements, the status of the player or players, timing, score, and so on. The rules are embedded in the application and the game does not have to rely on the player following them; it can enforce them instead. The programmer has complete power of decision about what information to display to the user and what information to hide. This choice needs to be used wisely. Too much information can render the game confusing, while too little can prevent the user from making the right decisions in the game.

Digital games are automated complex systems. They allow the programmer to automate complicated procedures, an obvious example being integrating the game rules, as stated above, into the program functionality. This facilitates the creation process and allows for some games to be implemented that would be difficult in a material version. The automation process can also hide the internal functionality of the game, and by not revealing why things happen a certain way, increase the player's disposition to suspend their disbelief.

An important aspect of digital games is the *networked communication* and the ability to allow multiple players to play a game together without having to be in the same room physically. This form of communication enhances the interaction in the game, being an addition to the actions available to the player. Experience shows that the communication between players is not limited to game play in those cases, which is why those game taking advantage of this communication also present a social aspect. This often leads to communities forming around some multi-player games.

2.2 Game Goal

If we see the game as a state system, then we can describe the *goal* or *objective* of the game as a particular state in the game that we want to reach or a particular property of the game state that we want to achieve. The goal can be *simple*, as in Tic-Tac-Toe or reaching a target in a maze. In other cases it can be *hierarchical*, consisting of a set of sub-goals or intermediate steps, as for example, in a first person shooter game. In other cases, the goal can eventually be just playing the game for the longest time possible and getting high scores, such as in Tetris.

Deciding on the goal of the game is arguably the most important part of the game design. This is what defines the game, and without a clear goal, the program can be seen as a toy instead of a game.

A goal that is too easy to achieve will not present enough of a challenge to keep the player interested for long. A goal that is too hard will discourage the player. Finding a middle ground is a challenge in itself, but the best kind of goal is the one that requires or allows the player to develop a strategy.

We can define a *strategy* as a plan, a sequence, or system of sub-goals that can take the player incrementally towards the game of the goal or that increases the chances of winning the game.

A special case of game goal is represented by game *levels*. These can be described as self-contained sub-environments, each of them with a defined goal. The purpose of the game in this case becomes to move up in the level hierarchy. They usually represent an ascending sequence in game difficulty, although many exceptions can be encountered where a difficult level is followed by an easier one. They are a nice way to demonstrate the player's proficiency with the game., as well as to organize the learning curve in the game.

2.3 Rules

The second most important thing defining a game is the *rules*. To cite another game theoretician, J. Huizinga, states that "The rules of a game are absolutely binding and allow no doubt."

The game must define the rules explicitly in a manner that is unambiguous. These rules are then shared by all the players involved and they are totally binding for the duration of the game. They are repeatable from one session to the next and even within the same session, similar rules apply to similar situations.

They define the player's actions threefold:

- what the player *can* do; these are *permissive* or *affirmative* rules; they define the space of possibility of action for the player;
- what the player *must* do; these are *binding* rules; they delimit the space of possibility of action, and
- what the player *must not* do; these are *forbidding* or *limiting* rules.

Let's take the game of Tic-Tac-Toe for an example. A permissive rule states that the player can place their token – and x or a 0 – on any open tile of the 3x3 board when it is their turn. A binding rule states that the player must make a move when their turn comes. A forbidding rule states that the player must not play more than one token, nor replace an already existing token on the board.

To explore the other side of the spectrum, let's look at

some of the rules in a role playing game (RPG). A permissive rule states that the player controls a character that they can move around on a 3 dimensional terrain in any direction. A binding rule states that the character moves must obey the laws of gravity (in most cases), so that the character's position must be bound to the terrain's altitude. A forbidding rule states that a player cannot mount a vehicle while engaged in combat. Note that the binding and forbidding rules are in this case embedded in the program. Thus, the player doesn't need to do anything special to follow them; the program will not allow him or her to do otherwise.

Thus, in digital games, the rules can and must be embedded in the program in a seamless way. Rules in the material world can simply become *outcomes* of actions in the digital world and the distinction is not always clear.

The permissive rules define the way the interface reacts to the user's actions: what objects should interact with the mouse or even the keyboard, what keys define the movement of the player's avatar and how they affect the player's interaction with the environment or with other players. In a board game of chess, a permissive rule states that the player can move any of their pieces in an allowed fashion when their turn comes. In a digital game of chess, when it is the player's turn, the pieces belonging to him or her would become interactive, the color of their outline changing, for example, when the mouse hovers over them. This example also emphasizes the need for the program to make it clear to the player what the possibility of action is by highlighting the elements of the game that allow for interaction and making them stand out somehow.

The binding rules become outcomes of the player's actions. In a board game of shoots and ladders, a binding rule says that if you arrive on a case that send you back on the trail, you must move your token accordingly. In a digital version of the game, the program can and must move the token automatically to the required position, in a way that is clear for the player to observe.

The forbidding rules are the negative space in a digital game and don't often need to be explicitly implemented. Everything that the player can do in a game needs to be implemented in the program, so a forbidden action can simply not be executed. For an example of an exception, a rule preventing players from traveling outside the boundaries of the realm in an RPG can be implemented more elegantly by having either insurmountable walls or expanses of water with an "exhaustion" feature added to them, activated when the player travels too far outside the zone. This way the world does not have to appear limited, even though it is.

In addition to the basic game functionality rules, there are implicit rules that the players are expected to follow, that we can call *good sport* rules. For example, in a turn-based board game such as chess, a player should make the next move within a reasonable amount of time. This is actually an explicit rule in chess tournaments, but it is also expected in casual play. After the given thinking time, the player is obligated to make a move or declare forfeit. Another example is the fact that the player is forbidden to take some action preventing the opponent from making a move, such as hiding the board or hitting the player.

Let's examine some of the implicit good sport rules in a multi-player role-playing adventure game. Helping players in the same faction when they need it is encouraged; they might even return the favor. Not fighting players in an opposite faction when they are at a much lower level or under-numbered. This second rule has been made explicit in some games such as World of Warcraft by the honor system. Being reasonably communicative also has a positive impact on the playing experience, but over-loading the general chat with unrelated content is sometimes considered rude. Using polite language is encouraged, and such games have language filters for this purpose. Treating other player fairly in trades. Some of these rules are actually stated in game contracts.

2.4 Playing a Game

We can define the game play in general as making choices based on the state of the game elements available to our perception and taking actions. Informally, these actions are called *moves*. We can describe playing as a loop where the player

- assesses the situation or state of the game;
- makes a plan;
- takes an action and observes the consequences.

Any such move has or should have consequences in the game, otherwise it has no purpose. The game is meaningful when the actions taken by the player have outcomes that are *discernable* in the game: the result of the action must be visible to the player. For this, the program needs to provide appropriate feedback. Even if a move a player is trying to make is not possible, and thus does not have consequences, a short audio alert can let the player know that they were doing something wrong. The move outcome must be integrated in the larger context of the game: an action taken at one point may affect the play experience at a later point in the game.

To enter the game play, the user must agree to a

"suspension of disbelief". This means that they must accept the world of the game to be real for the duration of the game and they must accept to play by the rules. Even though these rules offer a restrictive path to the goal, the players accept their limitations because of the pleasure the game can afford.

For the game play to work and the player to have the feeling that they are making meaningful choices, the program needs to convey some information properly. First, the situation in the game before the player was given the choice to make a move and the events that led to it. Second, the choices of action available to the player; a failure to do so will leave them not knowing what to do. Third, the player's move must have an immediate effect at the level of the interface, to let them know that they did take the intended action. Any other consequence of the action must also be made apparent. Failure in proper action – outcome connection at the level of the interface can result in players losing a game without understanding why, which can lead to them not playing it again.

We can identify several components of the game playing experience. *Visual scanning* is the visual perception of the game elements. *Auditory discrimination* consists of listening to the game events and signals. *Motor responses* are the physical actions taken by the player with the game controls. *Concentration* is simply the degree of focus on the game. *Perceptual learning* happens when the player assimilates the structure of the game and develops a strategy.

2.5 Special Cases

Here are some special cases of games that don't quite fit the general description for rules and game play.

21

Let's start by examining the idea of *toy* versus game. There is a similarity between them, mostly in the fact that they are both designed for entertainment. They are also both symbols for something else. For example, a toy car is a symbol for a real car. The difference becomes clear when we note that a toy is intended for informal, casual interaction, not governed by specific rules. The boundary between playing with a toy and not playing with it is not as clear. A game is either played or not, while a child carrying a toy with him or her everywhere may or may not be playing with it at any particular moment. The most obvious difference is the lack of defined goal.

Puzzles are a games for which there is usually a single path to the game goal, or otherwise, a single correct answer. The challenge consists in finding it.

Role playing games (RPGs) allow the player to control and evolve a character over time in a narrative setting, gaining in level and skills through quests or combat. This type of game is special in that it is difficult to define a quantifiable outcome for it. It is the best example of the principle that the journey is more important than the destination.

Games such as *Sim City* and *Farmville* have no explicit goals, other than sometimes in the shape of individual quests. The term often used for them is "sandbox games" because they let the player build a personal environment out of available building blocks. In terms of games theory, we can classify them as toys rather than games, even if not in practice.

Chatterbots, such as Eliza or the recently famous Cleverbot, can also be thought of as toys.

2.6 Games as Systems

A symbol is an entity that represents something, either an object, or an idea. For example, a coin represents an amount of gold residing in a bank, and it counts as an object. For an idea, we can look at a traffic sign representing a driving rule to be followed. Games are highly symbolic in nature, many of them representing a real-life conflict situation.

First, we have the game *tokens* which are symbols that stand for real objects, such as vehicles, guns, soldiers, and so on. These are the objects in the game that can be acted upon during game play. Second, we have the game *moves*, which are also symbolic actions that can be related to real actions on objects represented by the game tokens, but that only happen in the context of the game. Third come the game *rules*, defining the possibility of action. Finally, the game goal is also symbolic.

To take this idea to the next abstract level, we can also see games as *systems*. Generally, a system is defined as a group of interacting, interrelated, or interdependent elements forming a complex whole. The objects in the case of a game are the tokens, or pieces, the players, and eventually the board, or more generally, the environment. These objects have attributes, such as the initial position and direction of movement. The entire set of their values at every moment represents the *state* of the system. These objects are in relationships established by the game rules, which determine how the objects affect each other. Finally, the environment of the system is the game being played and the social context around it.

The best description for a game would be as a dynamic system. A more interesting question is whether a game is an open system or a closed one. Many games can be seen as closed systems, as they are completely described by the game objects and rules, and by the player's actions. There are exceptions, such as the game of Poker, where an external entity, the currency at stake, influences the game play.

A game can also be seen as a system with states, in many cases a large but finite number. An action from the player moves the game or system from a state to another state.

Another side of this story is that games are systems of information or information manipulation. As such, we can classify them based on how much information is available to the player. *Perfect information* games are those where all players have complete knowledge about every element of the game at all times. A good example is the game of chess. *Imperfect information* games are those where some of the information may be hidden from players during the game. An example is a Poker game where each player has a hand of 5 cards that are hidden from the other players.

We can distinguish the *objective* versus *perceived* information. Sometimes a player can have the impression of knowing more than they actually do. Even in a game of chess, a player can see all the pieces on the table, but may not play attention to a particular dangerous configuration. Even though everyone is playing the same game, we can identify the information known to all players, known to one player, known to the game only, especially for digital games, and randomly generated.

2.7 Interactivity

Let us examine the interaction in the game more closely. The term is defined as a mutual or reciprocal action or influence. It allows a two-way flow of information between two entities that can result in some change of status. There are many things that are now called interactive, such as an "interactive book". Does the term really apply to all of them, or is it sometimes used as a buzz word?

We have already discussed the most important type of interaction in a game, which is *playing the game*. As mentioned, this consists of making choices of action within the game system in order to achieve the goal. Thus, we can now see a game as an interactive system and the player as an agent within it, capable of generating action and change the state. We can call this type of interaction with the game objects *formal*. This explicit player interaction makes the game advance and defines the game experience.

A less obvious interaction happens during game play at a *cognitive* and interpretive level: the psychological, emotional, and intellectual perception of the game. It is related to the player learning the game and becoming better at it with accumulated experience. It also involves rational and emotional elements that will make him or her play the game again. It is important for a game designer to give the players reasons to come back to the game even after they have seen all or most of the available content. This is sometimes known as the "replay value" of the game.

The second type of interaction is *social* and summarizes all the informal exchanges with other players within the game. It is not limited to the temporal extent of the game; some players continue discussing the game even after it is over. We can include here the *cultural* participation in the game through online groups and forums, taking part in conventions, as well reading or writing literature related to the game content.

2.8 Games and Uncertainty

Randomness is a central feature in most games, necessary to give the player a feeling of purpose. We can identify the uncertainty element at two levels: in the general outcome of the game, and at the level of each move that depends on chance. For the first level, this means that the player does not know from the start whether the game will be won or not, otherwise there would be little interest in playing. For the second level, in many cases, the player makes the choice of a move based on estimation of the outcome, without having a certainty about it.

The uncertainty of a move's outcome can have several sources. The most obvious one is in games such as backgammon or role-playing card games where dice are used to determine the outcome of a move, or their digital equivalent. For sport games, such as golf, it is related to the amount of physical control the player has over his or her movements while hitting the ball. We can also consider in that case the contribution of other factors that cannot be completely known, such as wind gusts and bouncing properties of the terrain. For other games, such as chess, it seems that the state of the game before and after the move are completely known. The uncertainty here comes form the difficulty to plan ahead over several moves or to predict what the opponent is going to do.

For an action-outcome couple, we can also identify several

degrees of uncertainty. At one extreme we have complete certainty, which is a situation that can occur sometimes. For example, if in a game of chess we make a move that will put the opponent in check mate, then the outcome of this particular move is certain. At the other extreme we have total uncertainty. Although this is possible in a game, if the player does not have any means to predict the outcome of a move, then developing a strategy becomes impossible and the game is meaningless. Most of the time, though, moves involve some amount of risk.

Another aspect related to uncertainty is the feeling the randomness that the players experience, their impression that things happen with a degree of randomness in a game. The general feeling of randomness is more important that the actual probability of outcome for each move.

2.9 Feedback in Games

Feedback is the information that the game provides the player after a move to inform him or her of the consequences of the move and whether it was a good choice or not.

Negative feedback penalizes the player for taking some action or failing to take appropriate measures to prevent some negative outcome, such as losing health or a life. *Positive* feedback rewards the player for achieving some sub-goals in the game, such as finishing a level, or for taking an action that facilitates the advancement towards the game goal, such as consuming a health-enhancing item.

A good balance of negative-positive feedback is necessary in the game to make it interesting. Shaping the conditions for positive and negative feedback and game losing and winning is essential in the game design. Each of these has a role in creating appealing game play.

Negative feedback stabilizes the game, as it makes the players think more carefully about the actions they take and better plan their moves. Positive feedback may destabilize the game by rendering the players over-confident.

Negative feedback can prolong the game by making it harder to achieve the goal. Positive feedback may hasten its end by the opposite. Neither of these effects is a good thing or a bad thing in itself. The difficulty of achieving the goal is a parameter that needs fine-tuning because the player can lose interest in a game that is either too easy or too hard.

Positive feedback stresses the importance of successes happening early in the game and this encourages the player to continue. Negative feedback magnifies late successes by making the goal seem more valuable as it was harder to reach and obstacles had to be overcome on the way.

Feedback can "accidentally" emerge from your game as an artifact of combination of actions that the game designers have not thought of. Such strategies or shortcuts are usually discovered and exploited by the players. It is important to identify them and decide whether to allow unintended effects to persist in the game or not. For example, in a popular multi-player RPG, a combination of healing oneself and freezing the adversary rendered one particular character class virtually undefeatable in player versus player mode. The features were adjusted in one of the patches to remove the unfair advantage over the other classes.

Feedback systems can take control away from the player by either enhancing or diminishing the effect of their actions in unexpected ways. It is also important for the game designer and producer to acquire feedback *from* the players and correct issues that hinder the game play.

2.10 Games and Conflict

Conflict is an intrinsic element of any game, even when it is not obviously so. Games offer a *staged* conflict, taking place within the confines of the game world and following the rules of the game. When there isn't a direct conflict between the player and critters in the game, an implicit conflict is still present between the player and the difficulty of achieving the game goals. Various types of conflict can be encountered over the game spectrum, oftentimes even within the same game.

According to the number of persons involved, we start with single player conflicts, such as can be observed in a puzzle game. This type of conflict is often called player versus environment. A similar conflict involving several players in a *collaborative* setting can also be present in such games, although it is a more common feature of more complex role-playing games. Even in such a setting, the cooperating players can still be competing for some of the resources.

On the other side we have games pitting players against each other in a *competitive* setting. These conflicts go from a single player versus a single opponent, to multiple players each on their own against each other, and to competing teams ultimately combining collaborative and competitive settings. For digital games, most of the time these settings require some form of networking features in the applications. However, two or more players operating the same console or machine are still relatively common. Outside of the digital world, sports often involve competing teams of players.

Creating conflict in a game is one way to keep the players interested. The most obvious way is to allow multiple players to play the game simultaneously. A persistent high score list, either local or online, will entice the player to try and beat it. Carefully designing the obstacles that the players can face on the way to the goal is also part of designing the conflict, as well as deciding if the players can overcome obstacles together, or whether they are playing against each other. In other words, should the structure of the game allow the players to have direct conflict or are there any resources for which they compete?

2.11 Game Design

Game design is defined as "the process by which a designer creates a context to be encountered by a participant, from which emerges meaning" (Salem & Zimmerman, 2004). It consists of designing both the structure and context in which the game takes place.

Creating a game means creating a structure that will play out in complex and unpredictable ways, a space of possible action that players explore as they take part in the game. The designer must craft a system in which the actions have meaning in support of the play of the game and do not distract or interrupt its play.

Successful games require a team with well defined roles for each person, or a programmer who is also competent in the other necessary aspects. Let's examine some of the roles that team members can have.

The *project manager* supervises the entire project, decides on the stepping stones in the process of writing the program, assigns tasks to team members, and makes sure that the creation process advanced at the desired pace.

A *graphical artist* will be needed to create the visual artwork used in the game, such as critter icons, textures, and animation. A *sound artist* will be needed to create the sound effects and music in the game. It is important that both of these aspects be coherent in and of themselves, and with each other. It would not be fitting for a grim realistic shooter game to be accompanied by cartoon sound, unless it's a deliberate choice for comic effect.

A *writer* must create the virtual context in which the game is played and the background story. For simpler games, this person could be the level creator. For more complex games, whole dialogs and narratives may have to be created to make the game complete.

The *programmers* in the team will put together all of the resources and implement the application using the language and API that were chosen for it.

Finally, during and after the implementation phase, the game will need to be tested. It is important to test the various components of the program as soon as possible, but a set of *game testers* will have to play the finished game and verify if it accomplishes the goal of meaningful play, if it has replay qualities, if it can keep the player interested, as well as test for any artifacts that can occur from the game rules that were not planned for.

Dana Vrajitoru

3. Elements of Game Implementation

In this chapter we discuss a few implementation aspects that are common to most games. Some of these ideas will be seen in practice in the chapters that follow.

3.1 Game Objects

What we call game objects are all the entities composing the game. We can classify them in different categories based on their functionality. Thus, they can be active, decorative, or interface objects. They are defined by properties or attributes and methods that allow for their manipulation.

Active objects are those that make the game happen. They are often animated and they react to events. If such objects are mobile or even animated at the level of the shape, we call them *sprites*. If they also present autonomous behavior, then we can call them *critters* or *characters*. A special name is reserved for characters that are not involved in combat, but rather provide information and dialog for quest purposes: non-player characters, or *NPCs*. Resource types of objects, that can be animated but lack autonomous behavior, are called *tokens*. In this category we can also find static objects that are active in the game in that their presence has an influence on the choices and events in the game. For an example we can cite walls and furniture, as long as they prevent movement through them.

The player is often represented by a special character or avatar. It is often associated with a number of lives, which can be lost or gained by actions in the game. The characters must interact with each other and with the player's character and their actions have global consequences. Certain actions in the game may generate new characters or delete existing characters. Killing a critter clearly results in its object being deleted in the code. Catching a power-up object in a game of Pong, for example, can grant a tripling of the active balls. In this case, the action resulted in two more sprites being created.

Decorative objects are sometimes called Graphic (Flash) or Backdrop objects. They don't interfere with the game. They are all the environment objects for which no collision detection is necessary. The term of *interactive geometry* versus non-interactive geometry is used to distinguish the static active objects from the purely decorative objects. Decorative objects can be animated if the game is visually ambitious. Examples include billboards, background movies, vegetation, etc.

Interface objects are those who do not have an active role in the game, but rather serve an interaction purpose, such as buttons and menus. A common name for them is *widgets*. While many APIs, such as Flash, provide a library of ready-to-use widgets, an ambitious game will want to create its own unique widgets, as this will help set it apart from other applications.

3.2 World Representation

What we call the *environment* is the description and representation of the realm in which the game takes place. It has a *spatial* quality, characterized by the number of dimensions and by boundaries. Distances and positions can be measured in the environment, either in integer or in real values.

The world we mention here is the collection and

organization of all the objects in the game together with the game environment. There are three classic representation types for the world: implicit, explicit, and by zone. The choice between them must be made quite early in the game as it will greatly influence the interactions between objects, especially the collision detection. These categories are based on how the interactive objects are stored in the environment representation, and the other way around.

Implicit World

In an implicit world, if the game requires an explicit spatial representation of the environment, then this representation does not store the active sprites in the game. More precisely, it does not associate each available spatial cell in world with the objects present at that location, but rather stores the sprite location within the representation of the sprite itself. The environment is just a repository of non-interacting game components. An example where such a representation is appropriate is a shooter game in the style of Asteroids.

In an implicit world, all the interactive objects must be tested for collision against all the objects in the game for which the interaction is meaningful. There is no easy way to limit these computations for this type of representation. For this reason, it is used in cases of low object density, where the number of objects is small enough for the extensive collision detection not to slow the game down visibly.

Explicit World

In an explicit world, the spatial environment is represented explicitly by a data structure, such as a table. This approach is appropriate for games where each cell of the space can have specific properties, such as being a wall, or a gem, or a piece of food. The world representation in this case is much heavier than for implicit worlds. For this reason, it is a good choice for games taking place in a small world with relatively high character density. Examples include games like JewelQuest and PacMan, and most likely any game involving a maze.

In this kind of world, most of the interactive objects are explicitly stored as part of the environment. For example, a maze can be a two-dimensional table with cells of an enumerated type to denote walls, spaces, or game tokens. The objects that have a life outside of the table can be easily mapped onto the closest table cell based on their coordinates. Thus, for each object, it is easy to select the interactive objects in its vicinity and detect the collision with or limit any other type of interaction to this subset only. This reduces the collision computations to the minimum necessary.

Zone-Based World

This third option is a compromise of the first two models and is the most common choice for complex games, with large worlds and many objects. Examples include any three-dimension first person shooter (FPS) game or role-playing game (RPG). It is an art and an achievement of any such game to make the zone transition seamless to the player.

In this model, the environment is structured in geographical (spatial) zones or subdivisions. Each zone contains a linked list of references to the objects present in it, or a more specialized container as the case might be. Any active object in the game, including the player, has knowledge of the zone they are in and they must register with the zone's manager on arrival.

With this representation, we only need to test the collision between all of the objects registered with each zone, or sometimes in adjacent zones, if the objects are close enough to the zone border. This reduces the collision computations to a manageable amount.

3.3 Events in a Game

Games are quite often good examples of *event-driven applications*. Such programs can be described as functioning on an endless loop where they capture an event and react to it. Thus, the process of designing and writing the program consists of writing all the functions that must be called in response to events that are relevant to the game, or otherwise said, the *callback* functions.

Many of the recent APIs that are popular in the game coding community, including those for mobile devices, are implemented on the basis of the event-driven model, providing easy and convenient ways to connect user-defined functions or classes with events. ActionScript 3.0 is such an example, and we will see this principle applied in practice in the applications discussed in later chapters.

Generally, the event loop in a graphical user interface (GUI) can be described as follows:

```
while (true)
{
    event = getNextEvent();
    callback(event);
}
```

The application is based on cycles of action and consequence. The system is in idle state between the events. A special case consists of timer events. Typically these are triggered at regular intervals by a dedicated object or callback function. The best way to understand timers is to think of timer events as any other events in the application.

Let us examine the types of events that can occur in a game and the kind of reaction that is typical to them.

Internal events are related to the processing of the user's actions and of their effects, or of any change of state in the game resulting from its normal progression as a dynamic system. Such events can be, for example, collisions happening as a result of objects in the game moving based on velocity. We can also consider ongoing changes in object attributes in special situations, such as explosions fragmenting objects and scattering them. In the same category we can count any change of status of sprites with autonomous behavior. As an example, we can look at the ghosts in PacMan, that are not just moving based on the current speed, but also following the player around.

A special category of internal events consists of *system* events. Every application on any system must be able to react properly to commands received from the operating system. These include to close down, to move out of focus (to the background), and to reactivate or come back in focus. A less obvious system event is launching the game, which is an action originating from the operating system of the device. Normally these are not the responsibility of the programmers, since most advanced APIs provide automatic inherited behavior that takes care of them. However, special callback functions can be defined in many APIs for special actions to be taking on launch and on exit. If that is the case, then the application needs to define its own versions of such functions prescribed in the library's documentation. For example, in ActionScript 3.0, the application can define loader classes or load class methods that can be called to perform special actions while the program is loading.

External events are mostly related to the direct interaction of the player with the program. This interaction happens either to make a choice (or a move) in the game, or to change the basic program functionality and settings. The collection of all such events, their callback functions, and the objects that have an interactive purpose in the application can be summarized the *interface* of the game.

3.4 Mathematical Foundations

Many games require a set of mathematical functions of properties as an underlying foundation to the good functioning of the game. The first thing we can include here is everything related to the geometry of the game objects and their interaction, as well as the physical laws of motion that apply to the object animation.

The mathematical rules of the game may sometimes seem trivial, but they are still present and it is important to understand them properly in order to write the code correctly. Some textbooks, such as (Salen & Zimmerman, 2004), refer to them as *operational rules*.

To start with a very simple example, let's take the game of Tic-Tac-Toe, where two players alternate marking the empty squares of a 3x3 board, the first one with Xs, the other one with Os, until one of them has 3 marks in a row and wins. The game board can be interpreted as a matrix or table containing integer values that we can code as 1 for empty cells, 0 for the player 0, and 1 for player X. If all the spaces are filled and there is no winner, the game ends in a draw.

The game starts with a table containing the value -1 in all the cells. A player can replace a -1 with the number (or token) belonging to them anywhere in the matrix. They take turns doing this. Let's describe the "3 in a row" state of the game that leads to a win, assuming that the indexes in the table start from 0. This state occurs if we can find in the table at least 3 cells containing the same value 0 or 1, let us label them with the row and column numbers (r_i, c_i), $i = 0,1,2$, such that one of these conditions is true:

$r_0 = r_1 = r_2$ (horizontal case) or

$c_0 = c_1 = c_2$ (vertical case) or

$r_i = c_i = i$, for $i = 0,1,2$ (main diagonal) or

$r_i = i$ and $c_i = 2-i$, for $i = 0,1,2$ (secondary diagonal).

For a more complex example, let us consider a game where sprites move based on velocity. If the acceleration is constant, and P is the position of an object in one frame of the game, then in the next frame the position will be

$$P' = P + v \, \Delta t$$

where Δt is the time lapse between the first frame and the second and v is the velocity vector.

If some acceleration is present (a), such as gravitational,

40

then the position in the next frame can be computed as

$$P' = P + v\,\Delta t + \tfrac{1}{2}\,a\,\Delta t^2$$

and the velocity in the next frame is

$$v' = v + a\,\Delta t$$

3.5 Game Loop

This is the essential component of any game. It is similar to the classic event-based GUI loop. It would seem like for many games, some things need to happen in between the user interaction events. However, if we treat timer events like all the other events, the usual event loop still applies.

For continuous animation, the callback function for the timer event is the most important aspect of the loop and determines the functionality of the game. Typically, this function is called **nextFrame** or **gameUpdate** or something similar, and the structure can be described as

```
function nextFrame()
{
    updateObjects();
    resolveInteractions();
    redraw();
}
```

For distributed applications where objects might run independently in their own thread of execution, each thread or each object defines its own independent loop.

If several objects are animated with their own timer, the overall game timer must be the greatest common divisor of all the object timers. But the best way to handle such a situation is to write an update function for each object that depends on the time lapse between subsequent frames, mentioned before as Δ*t*. This takes the application closer to a realistic physics engine.

3.6 Animation Type

By animation we mean any change to the state of the game that results in visible effects in the application window. Ideally, the animation should happen fast enough for the human eye to perceive it as continuous. Such changes include the position of all the objects in the game, internal properties of objects, such as mouth opening phase for a PacMan, or background color and theme.

Practically, the animation can be described as composed of *frames* or *cycles*. These correspond to the sequence of calls to the function **nextFrame** or **gameUpdate** mentioned in the previous section.

The simplest form of animation is found in the *reactive games* where changes happen only when the user interacts with the game. Puzzles are perfect illustrations of this concept.

The opposite of that is *continuous animation* where characters in the game have a continuous behavior, such that changes happen even in the absence of user input. As a subset of this, we can mention *distributed animation* where the behavior of each character in the game is controlled by a different thread or timer in the program.

The next two chapters discuss these two types of animation in more detail and introduce a number of games for each of them.

4. Reactive Games

In this category we include any kind of game where the only changes in the game happen as a direct consequence of an action taken by the player. There are many examples of successful games that follow this mold, like all the puzzle games, and they may not always be the simplest kind of program to implement. In this chapter we'll look more in detail at some of the types of games in this category and at the challenges that they can present for the programmer.

We can describe reactive games by an iterative process as shown in Figure 1.

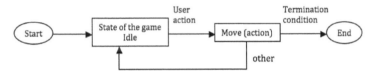

Figure 1. General description of reactive games

The game system is defined by a collection of objects: tokens, cards, tiles, or critters. The state of the game is the set of values of all the attributes of all the game objects at any given time. Reactive games can be described by the fact that the state of the system does not change unless an explicit action is taken by the user.

Thus, the game is in a loop where it waits for the player to make a move. Once that happens, a change is made to the state of the system based on what action the user has taken, and the game system is transitioned to another state. After that, the program must probably check for a termination condition, such as the game being on, or lost, or an explicit new game being started by the player.

4.1. No Memory Games

The simplest type of reactive game is one that we can call a "no memory game". In these games, the actions that the user takes are directly converted into changes to the state of the game, without the need to wait for a second action from the part of the player to complete the move. Figure 2 shows the general schema of these games.

Examples of such games include the hangman, mines, some puzzles, some card games like Golf, or even games with a player avatar like Gold Digger.

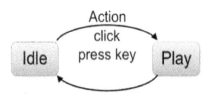

Figure 2. General schema for no memory games

In these games, a game transition is completely defined by the current state of the system and the player's action. All that is needed to perform the move is the current situation in the game, and the details of the user action - mouse position, key being pressed, or menu item being called. The program does not need to remember any of the previous states of the system than led to the current state, nor the previous actions taken by the player.

From a programming point of view, this means that the action function needs only one parameter, which is the most recent event. The function should be able to translate this into a game object identified by the event, as for example, the tile that the player has clicked on, and the type of action to be taken on it, if more than one is possible. For a mouse click, a key modifier can help select the action type, such as the shift being held during the click. A right-click versus left-click can also differentiate the action type.

Next, we'll go through the implementation of a no memory game in Flash ActionScript 3 step by step. The chosen game for this section is Mines, a popular game that originated on Microsoft Windows, but is now available on many platforms. Before we start working on the code, we need to have a general idea of how the game will be implemented and what the major components and data structures it will use.

Let's start with a brief description of this well known game. It consists of a tile table starting out with closed tiles. A given number of them placed randomly on the table are mines, all the others being safe (empty) places. If the player clicks on a mine tile, then the game is lost. If the player clicks on a safe tile, then all the safe tiles in its vicinity are opened, as well as all those in a contiguous safe region around the starting tile. Each opened tile is marked by a number counting the mines present in the adjacent 8 tiles. The game is won when all the empty tiles are opened without clicking on a mine.

Thus, the basic organizational structure is a 2D table, a simple rectangular matrix, containing all the tiles. In this game, the table will be implemented as a class containing an array of arrays, using the built-in class **Array**. We call this the container class.

The table could directly handle the tiles themselves, or they could be implemented as stand-alone objects of their own class. The second option facilitates the interaction with the mouse. Thus, we will have an independent object for each tile that handles the space in the game dedicated to that tile and the images that are displayed for it. This means that a mouse event can be associated with that object, such that a mouse click would directly spring that tile into action. This avoids a tile identification step that would be necessary if the table itself was responsible for the interaction with the mouse.

We have already discussed states of the system. Here we're extending the concept of state a little further, associating them with individual objects, and not only with the entire system. An object that has a state attribute can also transition from one state to another based on a game event. In this case, the entire behavior of the object is determined by the state; the same event or user action can have different consequences based on the object's state.

A tile can be in one of the following states: closed, flagged, exploded, and empty (opened). A tile object will own several images, or ActionScript sprites based on these images, and determine which one to display based on the state. A mouse event will be associated with the closed tile sprite, to allow it to either be opened or flagged. Another mouse event will be associated with the flagged sprite, allowing it to be un-flagged.

Whenever an empty tile is open, the tile needs to communicate with the table to let it know what happened. The tile itself is not aware of its neighbors, and thus, not capable of opening all the tiles in the contiguous empty area around it, nor of counting the mines in its vicinity. These operations must be done by the table, or the container class. On the other hand, when the table opens tiles in the area, it needs to send them a message to change from a closed state to an empty state. Thus, the tile class must store a reference to the container class, and the container class must store references to all the tiles. A tile must also store information about its position on the table, in order to be able to communicate it to the table when it sends it a message about being opened.

Figure 3 summarizes the two classes, the operations defining the game that each of them is responsible for, and the messages exchanged between them.

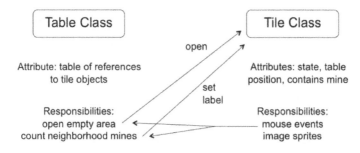

Figure 3. The two classes implementing the game of mines

Tutorial 1

Suppose that we want to implement a game of Mines, the simple game that you can find on Windows, with clones on other systems also available.

Let's start a new Flash / ActionScript 3.0 project called **mines**.

The basic structure that we're going to need is a table to contain the tiles in the game. We'll assume the "beginner" settings in the game where the table has dimensions 9x9 and there are 10 hidden mines.

Stage

The first thing to do is preparing the stage. We'll start with a square stage large enough to store 9x9 tiles, and with a border around it for other interface elements we might want to add. We'll assume that you're working in the Classic mode for the workspace. In the Properties area to the left of the stage, click on the Edit button next to the dimensions to make it 400x400, and then on the color square to set the background color to whatever you want.

Basic Images

Next, we need to create the following five tile objects: a closed tile, a highlighted one, a tile having a flag on top of it, a mine that has exploded, if the game is lost, and a bomb that has been revealed, when the game is won. Since these are easy enough, we'll create them using vector drawing directly in Flash.

Let's start with the closed tile. Start by drawing a square of 30 x 30 pixels in a color contrasting with the background, anywhere on the screen. For that, click on the rectangle tool, then click on the first corner, then drag it, and release for the second corner. Then click on the Selection tool (pointer) in the toolbar to the left of the stage all the way to the top, and double click on the rectangle you just created. Double click on it to select it. In the Properties panel to the right, set its width and height to 30. Set a border in a color contrasting with the background (darker or lighter), and then set the fill color of the tile as whatever you want. Then if you feel confident about it, you can add more decorations to it, for example, to give it a 3D effect.

Select the entire tile and make a copy of it somewhere close by. Edit the colors of the second tile to lighten them. This will be your highlighted tile to be used when you click on it. Once you've done that, select this entire second (highlighted) tile, right-click on it, then select Convert to Symbol from the pop-up menu. Leave the type of the symbol `MovieClip`, and give it the name `TileHighlighted`. Click on the button labeled Advanced and check the option Export for ActionScript.

Paste another copy of the first (simple) tile somewhere else, and then select the original first tile and convert it to another symbol of the same type called `TileClosed`. Then go back to the second copy of the original tile and add something that looks like a flag on top of it. Select the whole tile and convert it to a symbol called `TileFlagged`.

Repeat the operation to create another version of the tile containing an exploded bomb and a simple bomb. Call them `TileExploded` and `TileBomb`. At the end, convert the original tile also to a symbol and call it `TileClosed`.

Once you are sure you have adjusted the color of the stage to match the tiles, simply delete them from the stage.

Next we'll need to draw an area for the whole table. Since the tiles themselves are 30 x 30, you'll have to draw a rectangle of size 274x274 to include a 2 pixels border. Click on the rectangle tool and set the stroke in the properties to No stroke (for now), set the fill color as you like, then draw another rectangle in the middle of the stage. Select it using the selection tool, and then edit its properties in the panel to the right.

Set both the width and the height to 274. Then we need to give precise values to its starting position, so that we know how to place the tiles in the code. If we subtract 274 from 400 and then divide by 2, we get 68. Set both the origin x and origin y to 68. This will center the table on the stage in both directions. Then the origin point for the tiles will be 70x70 (we will add a 2 pixel border next). Now you can set the stroke of this area as 2 pixels wide and whatever color you want. Without deselecting it, right-click on it and convert it to a symbol. Since we don't need to interact with it, you can select the type of symbol as **Graphic**. This one does not need to be exported to ActionScript.

Tile Class

Now we can start coding. Let's create a class handling a tile. From the File menu, select New, then ActionScript file. Save it in the same folder, under the name **"Tile.as"**. Copy the following text into this file and save it:

```
package
{
    import flash.display.BitmapData;
    import flash.display.Sprite;
    import flash.display.Stage;
    import flash.utils.Timer;
    import flash.geom.Matrix;
    import flash.events.MouseEvent;
    import Math;
    public class Tile
    {
    }
}
```

The remaining of the code will go inside the pair of curly braces following the class name. First, we need to add some attributes that will store a sprite object for each of the five tile images that we created in the stage. Add the following line inside the class definition, right at the top:

```
var closedClip, highlightedClip, flaggedClip,
explodedClip, bombClip;
```

Then we need an attribute to tell us which of these states the tile is in, then another one to store the parent of the tile, which is the stage, since we need to reference it, and one to tell us if the tile is a bomb or not. We make this last attribute public because we might need easy access to it from outside of the class code. We need a couple of attributes to keep track of the table coordinates of the tile (row and column) and of its coordinates on the stage (x and y). Last, we would like to keep track of its size, so that we can reprogram the game easily with a different size for the tiles. We can assume that they will always be squares. So add the following list of attributes right under the first ones:

```
var parent, table;
var x, y, col, row;
var orgx = 70, orgy = 70, size;
public var state, isBomb;
```

Now add the following function that will take an instance of one of the clips that we created before and converted to symbols and position it within the tile object at the stage coordinates stored for the tile.

```
public function positionClip(clip)
{
    clip.x = x;
    clip.y = y;
}
```

Let us now write a function that initializes a tile. Add the following function above the previous one but below the declarations of attributes:

```
public function Tile(theStage, c, r, tab,
                     tileSize = 30)
{
    col = c;
    row = r;
    size = tileSize;
    x = orgx + r*size;
    y = orgy + c*size;
    parent = theStage;
    table = tab;
    state = 0;
    isBomb = false;
    closedClip = new TileClosed();
    parent.addChild(closedClip);
    positionClip(closedClip);
}
```

and the replicate the last 3 lines in the function for each of the clips we declared in the class, using their respective symbol class name that we entered for them when we converted the drawings to symbols.

Now we are ready to create a tile object and add it to the screen. Go back to the project file and open a window called Actions from the Window menu. Make sure that Layer 1: Frame 1 is selected in the left bottom area of the window. Then add the following two lines to it:

```
import Tile;
var t = new Tile(this.stage, 1,1, null);
```

Save all the files and then test the program with Ctrl-Enter. You should see the stage such as you've set it up, plus a tile on the top left, a little away from the corner.

First, we need to hide all the clips but the closed one. For this, add the following line to the initialization function:

```
highlightedClip.visible = false;
```

and then add a similar line for all the others.

Go back to the mines project file (with extension .fla) and open the Actions window. Let's add all the tiles now to the table. Replace the line declaring the variable t with the following:

```
var t;
for (var i = 0; i<9; i++)
{
    for (var j = 0; j<9; j++)
    {
        t = new Tile(this.stage, i, j, null);
    }
}
```

Now run the program again. If everything went fine, you should see all the tiles in the table, perfectly lined up with the background square.

Before we move forward, let us add a couple of functions to the class **Tile** that will be useful later. The first one is setting the bomb flag to true. The second one is setting the state of the tile to a particular value. For this, it first makes all the sprites invisible, then turns the one that is relevant to the new state to visible.

```
public function setBomb()
{
    isBomb = true;
}

public function setState(s:int)
{
```

```
    state = s;
    closedClip.visible = false;
    highlightedClip.visible = false;
    flaggedClip.visible = false;
    explodedClip.visible = false;
    bombClip.visible = false;
    switch (state)
    {
        case 0:
            closedClip.visible = true;
            break;
    }
}
```

Note that the code for setting the right sprite as visible is only provided for the first case. Complete the function with four other cases for each of the clips. Remove all the instructions from the initialization function that make the clips visible/invisible, and replace them by a single call to the function **setState** with the parameter being corresponding to the initial closed state.

Before we move forward, we can remark that a parameter of 0 will not be very informative for the reader of the code, and we would have to go back to this function and remember what state each number represents. What we can do instead, is to declare some new attributes named after the states in which the tile can be, and use those instead of the numbers. We can make them public because we might need them from outside the class too. These are a substitute for the C++ enumerated types that are not supported by ActionScript. So let's add the following to the list of attributes:

```
public var closedSt = 0, highlightedSt = 1,
          flaggedSt = 2, explodedSt = 3,
          bombSt = 4, emptySt = 5;
```
Container Class

To complete this game, we need another class that will keep track and manipulate the entire mine field. This class will keep references to all the tiles so that when we click on one, we can count the bombs hidden in the neighborhood and display the information on the tile.

Create another ActionScript 3.0 class called **MineTable.as**. Add a "**package {**" block to it just like for the **Tile** class, and the following import statements inside:

```
import Tile;
import Math;
```

Add an attribute called **table**, another one called **size**, and one called **parent**. Copy the attributes from the class **Tile** listing all the states here, otherwise we'll need to access them every time through an object of the class Tile, which can be inconvenient. Now let's write the initialization function for the table, or constructor. The table itself will have to be a two dimensional array. We'll use the built-in class Array for this. Since this provides one dimensional arrays, we'll need to create an array of arrays.

```
public function MineTable(theStage, dim:int)
{
    var i, j;
    size = dim;
    parent = theStage;
    table = new Array(size);
    for (i = 0; i<size; i++)
    {
        table[i] = new Array(size);
        for (j = 0; j<size; j++)
        {

            table[i][j] = new Tile(parent, i,
                                   j, this);
```

```
        }
    }
}
```

Go back to the project file and replace the entire code of the two loops creating the tiles with the following line:

```
var t = new MineTable(this.stage, 9);
```

Test the program. If everything is fine, you should see the same configuration as before.

Let's add some bombs to the table. First, declare another class attribute called **bombsCount**. Then add the function on the following page.

The **random** function generates a random number between 0 and 1. By multiplying it by the **tilesCount**, we obtain one between 0 and the number of tiles left to examine. **bombsLeft** indicates how many bombs we still have left to place on the table. So, for each position on the table, we generate a random number between 0 and the number tiles left, and if that number happens to be between 0 and the number of bombs left to place, we make that tile a bomb. At the same time we decrease the number of bombs left to place, since we've placed one, and the number of tiles left to examine. This procedure gives each tile a chance to be a bomb equal to the total number of bombs divided by the number of tiles in the table, aiming to distribute them evenly in the table. This is based on a known algorithm that was proved to give every tile in the table the same probability to be turned into a bomb, while ensuring that we will place the exact count of bombs we need on the table.

```
public function setBombs(count)
{
    var i, j, u;
    bombsCount = count;
    var bombsLeft = count,
        totalTiles = size*size;
    for (i = 0; i<size; i++)
    {
        for (j = 0; j<size; j++)
        {
            u = Math.random() * totalTiles;
            if (u < bombsLeft)
            {
                table[i][j].setBomb();
                table[i][j].setState(bombSt);
                bombsLeft --;
            }
            totalTiles--;
        }
    }
}
```

What this function is not doing, though, is avoiding those situations where a bomb might be surrounded on all sides by other bombs, which normally is not a circumstance you should allow in the game. Even though this will happen rarely, some modifications to the function will have to be done to account for it. We will leave it up to the reader to think of a solution for this.

In the function above, for testing purposes, we have set the state of all the tiles that are turned into bombs as 4, which corresponds to the bomb clip. After testing it a few times, when you are satisfied that it works properly, you can comment out that part by placing two forward slash characters (//) at the beginning of the line. This is similar to C++ style comments. You can also delete the line instead, but it might be useful to have it there for easy access in case you want again later it for debugging.

Events

Now it's time to start making these tiles clickable. For that we need to attach a function to be called in case of an event, or a *callback* function, to objects in the scene that should react to a mouse click. The event here is the mouse click itself. In ActionScript we can attach the callback function directly to objects like sprites and movie clips, so that when a click happens, the object that the mouse pointer was over at that time will react by calling the appropriate function. This way we don't need to worry about relating the mouse position to objects on the screen and deciding which object the event applies to. In other APIs this is something that might have to be done by hand.

Let's think for a moment at what kind of interaction we want from our tiles. The only tiles that need to be clickable are the closed tiles. If they have been opened before or flagged, nothing should happen if we accidentally click on them. The way we've set up the tile symbols in the project, when we click on a closed tile, its image should be replaced in a first stage by the highlighted one. Only when we release the mouse button, the action should take place. We already have a function that can make this change for us, which is the function **setState** with a parameter of 1. We just need to link this function to the event. First, let's create a function that will be called when the closed tile is clicked. In the **Tile** class, add the following function before the end of the class definition:

```
public function clickClosedTile(ev:MouseEvent)
{
    setState(highlightedSt);
}
```

and then go back to the constructor of the class **Tile** and add the following call at the end of it:

```
closedClip.addEventListener(
    MouseEvent.MOUSE_DOWN, clickClosedTile);
```

If you save the file and run the program again, when you click on the tiles, they should light up.

Game Functionality

Next, what needs to happen is that when the mouse button is released, the functionality of the game should be activated. We will define another callback function that we'll attach to the highlighted tile clip, with the event type being **MOUSE_UP** instead of **MOUSE_DOWN**. Then we need to figure out what should happen when we activate the tile. There are several cases to consider.

First, if the tile is a bomb, then we should fire it, and the game should be lost. For this, we should go through all of the tiles, and those that are still closed should be opened, either showing an empty space if they were empty, or showing the bomb image if they contained a bomb. A closed tile would normally be in a state of 0, but we could include the state of 1 to apply the same procedure to the tile that was highlighted. Here is a function to accomplish this that should be added to the class **MinesTable**:

```
public function fireAll()
{
    var i, j;
    for (i = 0; i<size; i++)
    {
        for (j = 0; j<size; j++)
        {
            if (table[i][j].state <= 1)
            {
```

```
        if (table[i][j].isBomb)
        {
            table[i][j].setState(
                        explodedSt);
        }
        else
        {
            table[i][j].setState(
                        emptySt);
        }
     }
   }
 }
}
```

Let's test this function right away. In the class `Tile`, add the following function:

```
public function
clickHighlightedTile(ev:MouseEvent)
{
    table.fireAll();
}
```

and then in the constructor for the `Tile` class, add the following line at the end:

```
highlightedClip.addEventListener(
    MouseEvent.MOUSE_UP,
    clickHighlightedTile);
```

Test the program and click on a tile. All the bombs should be shown, and all the other tiles should disappear.

Let's make the bombs only appear when we click on a bomb. Replace the function call to **fireAll** in the function **clickHighlightedTile** with the following conditional testing if the tile is a bomb:

```
if (isBomb)
{
    table.fireAll();
}
else
{
    setState(emptySt);
}
```

This way, if we click on an empty space, it just opens up. Otherwise, the bombs are fired. As an easy exercise, modify the function `fireAll` such that if a tile is flagged and it is a bomb, the bomb clip is displayed instead of the flagged or the exploded one. Thus, if the player loses the game, he or she will still find out how many bombs they have guessed.

Before we take care of the lengthier details related to clicking on an empty tile, we could deal right now with the flags. The easiest way to deal with them is to add the flag to a closed tile by holding down the shift key while clicking on it.

The function `clickHighlightedTile` takes one parameter that is the event. This parameter event is a complex structure containing a variety of data. One attribute that we can use here is the `shiftKey` that is true if we were holding the shift key down while clicking the mouse, and false if not. So let's add a test at the beginning of this function:

```
if (ev.shiftKey) {
```

and if this is true, then call the function `setState` with the parameter value equal to `flaggedSt`. Add an `else` before the `if` statement that was there already and make sure that the braces close appropriately.

Now that we've added the flags, we realize that we should be able to remove them. We want to remove them only if we click on those tiles again with the **shift** key held (we want to avoid accidentally setting up a flagged bomb). Add another function called **clickFlaggedTile**, make it call the function **setState** with the parameter **closedSt** if the shift key is held, then link it to the flagged clip with the event **MOUSE_UP** in the constructor for the **Tile**. Test the program to see if it works.

Text Box

We're almost there with the game. What we need to do next is two things. First, when we click an empty tile, we need to count the neighbors of that tile that are bombs and display a number on its tile. Second, when a tile is opened that does not have any neighboring bombs, all of its neighbors that are still closed should also be opened.

To be able to display these numbers, we need an object that can display text. We'll add it programmatically to the class **Tile**. Add an attribute at the top called **textBox**, and add the module **flash.text.TextField** to the list of imported modules at the top of the package (before the class definition). Then add the following lines to the **Tile** constructor, after all the clips have been added to the parent:

```
textBox = new TextField();
textBox.x = x+9;
textBox.y = y+9;
textBox.text = "4";
parent.addChild(textBox);
textBox.visible = false;
```

Comment out the line making the **textBox** invisible for testing. When you run the program, you should see a number 4 displayed on top of all the tiles. You can tweak the 9 added to the **x** and **y** of the text box to make it centered over the tile (9 has worked for me). Once you have done that, delete the 4 in the code you added, but leave the pair of quotes in place. This will initialize the text with an empty string, and then uncomment the line making the **textBox** invisible. The **textBox** needs to be invisible even though the text that it displays is empty, because if it is visible, it interferes with the functionality of the button.

We are ready now to write a function that checks all of the neighbors of a tile and counts the bombs. There are several different ways in which this can be accomplished. Our solution for this is to store two arrays that give us the offset in the two coordinates of each of the 8 neighbors. For example, the neighbor that is up and to the left of the current position will have an offset of -1 on both coordinates.

Add the following function to the class **MinesTable**:

```
public function countBombsAround(xTile, yTile)
{
    var offx:Array = [-1,0,1,1,1,0,-1,-1];
    var offy:Array = [-1,-1,-1,0,1,1,1,0];
    var i, count = 0, c, r;
    for (i = 0; i<8; i++)
    {
        c = xTile + offx[i];
        r = yTile + offy[i];
        if (0 <= c && c <size &&
            0<= r && r<size)
        {
            if (table[c][r].isBomb)
            {
                count++;
            }
        }
    }
}
```

```
    return count;
}
```

Then go back to the Tile class, in the function `clickHighlightedTile`, and add the following code after setting the state of the tile as empty:

```
var c = table.countBombsAround(col, row);
textBox.text = c;
textBox.visible = true;
```

Test the program to see if this works correctly. You should now be able to play a full game yourself by clicking on all the tiles that surround any tile marked 0.

As an easy exercise, make the tile display the number only when it is not 0. If you want to fine-tune your display, you can also set the color of the text based on the number. For example, adding the following code to the lines above, will display the digit 1 in green:

```
if (c == 1)
{
    textBox.textColor = 0x007700;
}
```

where 007700 is a hexadecimal representation of the color that is identical to the HTML code for colors. I will let you choose the other colors, if you want to do that.

The only thing left to do is to open all the tiles adjacent to the ones where the count of surrounding bombs is 0. The function will be similar to the one above, but it will have to call itself recursively. To avoid too many function calls, we also need to call the function open only those tiles that are still in a closed state.

First, turn the code that sets the text in the **textBox** based on a number, together with setting the color, into a function called **setTextBox** taking a parameter called **count**. Replace "c" in that code with the parameter **count**. Add an **else** to the main conditional in this function such that when **count** is 0, the **textBox** is made invisible. Add the following function to the class **MinesTable**:

```
public function openTile(xTile, yTile)
{
    var offx:Array = [-1,0,1,1,1,0,-1,-1];
    var offy:Array = [-1,-1,-1,0,1,1,1,0];
    var i,count = 0,c,r;
    count = countBombsAround(xTile,yTile);
    table[xTile][yTile].setState(emptySt);
    table[xTile][yTile].setTextBox(count);
    if (count == 0)
    {
        for (i = 0; i<8; i++)
        {
            c = xTile + offx[i];
            r = yTile + offy[i];
            if (0 <= c && c < size &&
                0 <= r && r < size) {
                if (table[c][r].state ==
                    closedSt)
                {
                    openTile(c, r);
                }
            }
        }
    }
}
```

This will be useful later when we restart the game.

Replace the entire code that handles opening the highlighted tiles that are not open yet with a simple call to this function

```
table.openTile(col,row);
```

Now the game should be fully functional.

Interface Elements

The game as it is, is a little bit bare. Let us add some interface elements to it, so that the player knows what is happening.

The first thing we would like to do is to add some text showing the number of bombs left to flag. First, add some text above the table in the stage with the caption "Bombs Left:". Use the text tool in the toolbar to the left of the stage to create this text, and set its type as Classic Text / Dynamic Text in the Properties area to the top right of the window. Give it the instance name "**bombsLeftText**". Set the font type, size, and color, the way you want. Make sure that the width of this text box will allow for a 2-digit number to be added to it. Create a similar one on the other side to display messages such as "Game Won" or "Game Lost". Give it the instance name "**gameWonText**".

Embedding Fonts

Click on one of these two text fields. In the Properties area on the right, you should see a button labeled Embed... next to the font name. Click on it. In the dialog that opens, check all the uppercase and lowercase letters, all the digits, and you can either check all the punctuation characters, or specify in the box below the ones that you think you'll need, like the exclamation mark and the period. Then click ok. Save your project. You need to embed a font to be able to see it in the **.swf** file.

Now we need to be able to access these instances from the **MinesTable** class. Add two attributes to this class called **bombText** and **gameText**. Add the following function to the class:

```
public function setTextFields(bt, gt)
{
    bombText = bt;
    gameText = gt;
    gameText.text = "";
}
```

Then go back to the .fla file, open the Actions panel, and after defining the table object t, call this function above the following way:

```
t.setTextFields(bombsLeftText, gameWonText);
```

Thus, even though we've defined these two objects in the stage, the table will now have access to them and will be able to modify the text that they display.

We already have a counter in the class **MinesTable** for the number of bombs on the table, initialized properly in the constructor. We need to add a counter for the flags, and a counter for the tiles that have been opened. Add an attribute called **flagCount** and another one called **openCount** and initialize both of them as 0 in the constructor. Then we need a function that will modify the flag count, updating the displayed text accordingly, keeping in mind that the count could go both up and down, since we allowed the player to remove flags too. Add the following function to the class:

```
public function addFlag(count)
{
    flagCount +=  count;
    bombText.text = "Bombs Left: " +
                    (bombsCount - flagCount);
}
```

Call this function with the parameter equal to 0 in the function `setTextFields` at the end. Then call it with a parameter equal to 1 in the function `clickHighlightedTile` in the class `Tile`, in the situation where a flag was added, the following way:

```
table.addFlag(1);
```

And last, call it again in the function `clickFlaggedTile`, in the situation where we remove the flag, with the parameter -1.

Let us now find out if the game was won or lost. It is easy to see if the game was lost: when the `MinesTable` class method `fireAll` is called. To mark it, we can set the text of the `gameText` attribute to "Game Lost" in this function.

For detecting a winning condition, first we need to count the tiles that are being open. In the function `openTile`, after opening the tile, we need to increment the `openCount` attribute. After that, if the number of open tiles plus the number of remaining bombs is equal to the total size of the table, then the game was won. Add the following code to this function, right after setting the text box of the tile based on the count and its state to empty:

```
openCount++;
if (openCount + bombsCount == size*size)
{
    gameText.text = "Game Won!!"
}
```

Button

Easy exercise: Add a button to the stage (that you can find under Components in the small area between the Stage and the Properties - you'll have to drag it to the stage) with the label

New Game and the instance name "**newGameBtn**". Add a function in the class table called **newGame**, with one parameter for the number of bombs on the table, in which you reset all the tiles as closed and without a bomb, and then call the function to generate a random bomb configuration again. You'll have to figure out which of the attributes that were initialized in the constructor need to be initialized again in this function.

Once you have this function, add the following code in the .**fla** file, after the code you already have there:

```
newGameBtn.addEventListener(MouseEvent.CLICK,
                           restart);
function restart(event)
{
    t.newGame(10);
}
```

This creates a function in the stage that is linked to the button we just defined, and that calls the new game function from the table.

Challenging exercises:

1. Set up your game in such a way that the player can choose the level of difficulty.

2. Modify the game such that when you click on a tile that has been opened and has a number on it, if the count of flags in it neighborhood is exactly equal to the counter written on the tile, all the adjacent tiles that are not flagged are opened.

4.2 Select One Object

This is a category of games that includes most card games where the player must select a card, then move it to another stack. It also includes jigsaw puzzles, chess, Sudoku, and most object matching games such as memory, Mahjong, and GemSwap. A general description of the main loop for these games can be seen in Figure 4.

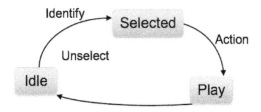

Figure 4. General schema for select one object games

In this type of game, the programming challenge comes from the fact that the player needs to perform an action on an object of the game in two steps: first, identifying the object, and second, identifying a second piece of information that is necessary to complete the action. While the actions in the no memory games were typically functions with one parameter, in the one object selection games, they take two parameters: the object that they apply to, and the current event. This is because an active game object can now have two states: selected or unselected. The kind of event generated by an action from the user will affect the object in a way that depends on its state. For example, an event of left click on the object itself while it is in a selected state will cause it to become unselected.

Let's examine what the object can be and what kind of

action can be applied to it. In a jigsaw puzzle game, for example, the actions taken by the user consist of moving the puzzle pieces around. This is accomplished by clicking on them and dragging them to the new position. The movement may seem to the user as a single continuous action, but from a programming standpoint, it is composed of three actions. The first one selects the object to move and highlights it, and is related to the mouse down event in the interface applied in the situation where no object has previously been selected. The second one is moving the object around while the mouse button continues to be down. This action is also attached to the mouse down event but in the situation where a selection is active. The third one places the object at the new position and is attached to the mouse up event.

For games where all of these actions are restricted to click-and-drag interfaces, and where the mouse events can be directly attached to the objects that need to react to them, like in Flash, these actions can be implemented the same ways as for no-memory games. They can be accomplished by changes in state of the objects.

But for many of these games, the functionality is implemented in a dual way: first, select the object that the action applies to, move the cursor to the new position without the mouse button down, and then click on the new position for the object to be moved there. In this case, the game needs to memorize the object that was selected in the first place, so that it can move it to the new position. Some card games are implemented this way: select a card, then the deck that it needs to move to. Another example would be the game of Bedazzled, where tiles are being swapped on a table to create 3 in a row. The swap can be done with a continuous mouse movement, or with a click to select, and then click to move to the new position.

For the situation where the game is implemented in an object-oriented way where each active token is represented by an object of a specialized class, it is possible to delegate the action entirely to this object. This can be done when the only possibility to perform the move is through mouse dragging. But for the other situations where we first click on the object, then on a place to move it to, multiple objects in the game will be involved in accomplishing the move. The selection process is connected with the object in the code representing the selected token. The second part of the action, though, will reference a different object in the code: the playing table for a game of chess, the destination stack of cards for a card game. Thus, in this situation, a game manager keeping references to all active game objects will have to be informed of the selected object in the first part of the move. In the second part, the game manager will need to coordinate the selected object with the destination of the move and send all the involved objects an appropriate message to finalize the action.

To give an example of this type of game, we will implement the Memory game. It consists in a table of card containing images that need to be remembered, two of each image. The game starts with all the cards facing down. The player can open two cards at a time. If the images match, then they remain face up or are removed. If they don't match, then they are turned back down.

Before we start the next tutorial, let us discuss the implementation details for this game. The organization of the program will be very similar to the mines game we've seen before, in that it is defined by two connected classes, one for a table, and one for the tiles.

The **Tile** class will have a similar structure to the one described in the game of mines. It will be responsible for a set of sprites built from imported images, and will have an attribute for a state that can be either opened or closed. A refinement of the game could include a third state, to distinguish between tiles that are opened in the process of matching them, and tiles that have already been matched and are permanently opened. An attribute will represent the image on the tile as an identification integer number. The objects will also store attributes for the position on the table, as well as a reference to the table object. A tile object will be responsible for handling mouse events. These can be directly attached to closed tiles sprites, since these are the only ones that need to react to the mouse click.

The table class will store a 2 dimensional array of references to tile objects and its main purpose will be to facilitate the communication between tiles and to organize the main functionality of the game. When a first tile is opened, some information about it will have to be stored in the table class, so that when a second one is opened, its identification number with the one of the tile previously opened. If the two of them are identical, then both tiles can be permanently opened. Otherwise both tiles will be closed. Thus, the communication between objects of the two classes needs to go both ways, for which reason each of them will store a reference to the other one.

The functionality of the **Table** class and implicitly that of the game is summarized in Figure 5. The rounded boxes represent states of the **Table** object. The hexagons represent tests. The "Select tile" action summarizes a mouse click on an open tile, followed by the tile object sending a message to the **Table** class informing it of the event, and identifying itself.

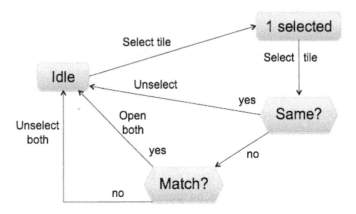

Figure 5. The functionality of the Table class

Tutorial 2

The following tutorial presents a step by step implementation of the Memory game.

Preparation

You'll need a collection of images that you want to use for your memory game. It's better to choose a theme for it. They need to be resized and cropped to the same dimensions. It's a good idea to have more images than you need, that way the game can be replayed without being too boring.

In addition, you need an image for the back of the cards, a frame for the front of the card to be displayed during the click action, one for the front of the card to show while you're looking for a match (let's call it active), and for the front of the card to show when a match has been found (let's call it solved). The frame for the active card displayed while you're looking for a match should be the one that catches the eye the best. Note that if the frames have some sort of border, then the content images (what the cards will display) need to fit on the frames in the space inside the border.

Figure 6 shows an example of the four card frames.

Figure 6. Examples of tiles images

Project

Create an ActionScript 3 project called memory. Make the size of the stage big enough to hold the table of tiles with the dimensions based on the size of your tiles and the count of cells. For example, if my tiles are of size 100 and I want a table of 4 rows by 5 columns, I will make the stage of size 520x450, adding a small margin on all sides. I am leaving more space beside the tiles vertically to add some replay buttons at the end eventually.

Details. In the Classic workspace, the stage size and color of the stage can be set in the Properties area to the left. Look for one of the Edit buttons.

Import images

You'll have to import your images one by one into the project and set their properties so that they can be used in the code. For this part you can select several files to import to the library in a single action, but I don't know any shortcut to turning them into classes that can be used other than one by one. From the File menu, go to Import and then to Library, then choose one or several of the images. Then open the library (small button to the left of the Properties area), right-click on the image you just imported, and select Properties. In the dialog that opens, check "Export for ActionScript" and rename the class as something you can easily remember.

For example, I will choose a name for each class based on the name of the file, modified to add the suffix "`Bmp`". For example, an image called `tileBack.png` generates the class name `tileBackBmp`. A warning about the class definition not being found will come up. Just click ok.

Class

We'll need two classes to implement this application: one to handle individual tiles, and another one handle the whole table of them.

Start by creating a new ActionScript file and save it under the name `Tile.as`. This will also have to be the name of the class. Start the file with

```
package
{
```

and end it with the matching }. Everything in your file will be in between. We will need to import some Flash classes that we'll be using. Just copy and paste the following in the file:

```
import flash.display.BitmapData;
import flash.display.MovieClip;
import flash.display.Sprite;
import flash.display.Stage;
import flash.utils.Timer;
import flash.geom.Matrix;
import flash.events.MouseEvent;
import flash.events.TimerEvent;
import flash.system.System;
import Math;
```

Below these, add the following lines defining the class `Tile`:

```
public class Tile
{
}
```

Next, we'll need to declare some attributes in this class. Each individual image that can be used by this tile will be stored in an individual sprite. We need five of these for the four tiles plus the image to be displayed on the front. Let's declare them as variables or attributes in the class like this:

```
var backSprite;
```

Underneath, let's add the following function that will take a parameter of type `BitmapData`, create a sprite out of it, and then return it. This function assumes that the size of the both the image that was imported and of the sprite to be displayed are `spriteSize x spriteSize`. We need this parameter because the frame sprites have different sizes. If the tiles are not square, you need to add another parameter to distinguish the width form the height. If the bitmap has a different size than the tile, a transformation matrix can be used to scale the image to the size of the sprite. We will see some examples in later tutorials.

```
public function makeSprite(bmpName, spriteSize)
{
    var sprite = new Sprite();
    sprite.graphics.beginBitmapFill(bmpName);
    sprite.graphics.drawRect(0, 0, spriteSize,
                                    spriteSize);
    sprite.graphics.endFill();
    return sprite;
}
```

This function creates a sprite, sets it up to be filled using a bitmap, then fills the rectangle specified on the third line with the bitmap. The coordinates are relative to the sprite position given by its **x** and **y** attributes.

Constructor

Next we'll write a function that defines how objects of this class are initialized. First, declare another variable in the class called **parent**. This will be a reference to the stage where all the objects will be displayed. Add the following function just above the first one:

```
public function Tile(theStage)
{
    var bmp;
    parent = theStage;
    bmp = new tileBackBmp(100, 100);
    backSprite = makeSprite(bmp, 100);
    parent.addChild(backSprite);
}
```

and replace "**tileBackBmp**" with the class name that you gave to one of the images that you imported before.

Testing the Class

Now we have enough information in this class to test if it works correctly and if we can display something on the stage. Go back to the project file and open the Actions dialog. Make sure Frame 1 is selected. Add the following lines that are importing the class Tile from the file and creating an object of this class. The expression "`this.stage`" identifies the display stage where everything is displayed.

```
import Tile;
var test = new Tile(this.stage);
```

To run the app, hit Ctrl-Enter. If there are no errors, you should see one tile in the top left corner of the stage.

Completing the Tile Class

If everything is working so far, we need to complete the tile class. Replicate the instructions for the first frame to create the four sprites for the four images. This is the easy part.

Next, add one parameter to the constructor function that will represent the image to be displayed on the tile when it is turned face up. This parameter is going to be an integer. Let's call it `option`; add it to the function as `(theStage, option:int)` to let Flash know that this is an integer.

To create the bitmap for it, we'll have to test its value and use a different class for each possible value. It's easier to do it in a separate function. This function will not be declared as public because it doesn't need to be called from outside the class. Start with the following structure:

```
function chooseBmp(option:int)
{
    var bmp;
    switch (option)
    {
        case 0 :
            bmp = new elekBmp(90, 90);
            break;
    }
    imageSprite = makeSprite(bmp, 90);
    parent.addChild(imageSprite);
}
```

and then replace "**elekBmp**" with the name of the class of your first image (the one you gave it in the properties). Also replace **90** with the size of your images. You'll have to add as many other cases in this function as the images you have. Once the function is finished, add a call to it at the end of the constructor, that looks like this:

```
chooseBmp(option);
```

Test that the code works so far by adding an option in code creating an object of the **Tile** class in the project Actions dialog and running it.

Placing the Tile

We need to add some functions to be able to place the tile at any position we want on the stage. This could be done in the constructor by adding a couple more parameters, but it would overcharge it. Besides, a separate function would allow us to re-place the tile later if we want to. Add the following code in the class:

```
function moveTo(spriteObj, valx, valy)
{
    spriteObj.x = valx;
    spriteObj.y = valy;
}
public function place(posx, posy)
{
    moveTo(backSprite, posx, posy);
}
```

Add a line in the function **place** for every sprite in the class. The frame sprites will have the same coordinates as the one shown above. The image to be displayed over the frames needs to be placed inside the frames, so its coordinates will be a little different. For this sprite, start from the tile's coordinates like for the others, then add an integer representing half of the difference between the size of the frames and the size of the images to both coordinates. This will center the image over the frame. For example, if the frames are of size 100 and the images 90, then you need to add 5 to both **posx** and **posy**.

Test this by calling the function from the code in the project file:

```
test.place(50, 50);
```

What to Display

Next we'll add a few functions that can be called to decide which frame sprite to display and whether or not to show the image sprite on top of them. We'll name the functions after each of the frame sprites. The first one will display the back frame without the image. Add the function on the following page to the class, and then replicate the function for the four other frame sprites, making only the appropriate sprite visible in each of them. For the **showLook** and **showFound** you also need to make the image sprite visible.

```
public function showBack()
{
    backSprite.visible = true;
    clickSprite.visible = false;
    lookSprite.visible = false;
    foundSprite.visible = false;
    imageSprite.visible = false;
}
```

Mouse Interaction

It's time to start making the tile react to mouse events. These events can and must be added to each individual sprite such that a function (callback) is called if any of them is clicked.

Let's start by adding a callback function to the back sprite. What needs to happen when a tile showing the back frame is clicked is to change it to a tile that was clicked. Add the following function to the class:

```
public function backClick(ev:MouseEvent)
{
    showClick();
}
```

Then we have to attach an event to the **backSprite** that captures the mouse being clicked. More precisely, we want the tile to be shown as "**clicked**" when the mouse button is down, and then opened when the mouse button is released. Add the following line to the constructor, at the end:

```
backSprite.addEventListener(
    MouseEvent.MOUSE_DOWN, backClick);
```

Test this functionality by going to the code in the project file and adding a call to the function **showBack** on the object **test** right after it is created. Then when you run the program and click on the tile, the "clicked" one should appear.

Add a similar function called **clickOpen** for the **clickSprite** where you call the function **showLook**. Instead of **MOUSE_DOWN** use **MOUSE_UP** to connect the function to an event.

Who/Where Am I

In the context of the whole game, the tile will be placed on a row and column in a table and it probably needs to know all this information and store internally. Let us declare three more class variables at the top (next to the sprites), and then declare a function that can be used to set them:

```
var row, col, theTable;
public function setPosition(r, c, tab)
{
    row = r;
    col = c;
    theTable = tab;
}
```

This is all the functionality we need in this class for now. Next we'll define a class handling the entire table of tiles.

Table Class

Create a new ActionScript file and call it **Table.as**. Inside it declare a package and then a class called **Table**. Copy the imported modules from the class **Tile** into this new one.

First, let us declare a variable in this class to store the table of tiles. This will have to be an array and we can declare it as one:

```
var table:Array;
```

Declaring the type of a variable or parameter in Flash doesn't affect the program but Flash can help you finding appropriate functions for it if you do.

Now we can define a function that initializes the tiles with random values such that there are two and only two tiles for each image type. The easiest way is to fill the table in order and then shuffle it. Let's start with the function **shuffle**:

```
public function shuffle(rows:int, cols:int)
{
    var i, r, temp;
    for (i = 0; i<rows*cols-1; i++)
    {
        r = I + Math.floor(Math.random() *
                           (rows*cols-i));
        if (i ! =   r)
        {
            temp = table[int(i/cols)][i%cols];
            table[int(i/cols)][i%cols] =
                table[int(r/cols)][r%cols];
            table[int(r/cols)][r%cols] = temp;
        }
    }
}
```

Basically this function chooses for each cell in the table a random position further down in the table and swaps the two cells. We find it easier to treat the table as linear by having i go from 0 to **rows*cols-1** and then compute the row and the column by dividing by the number of columns and by applying the modulo (%) operation respectively.

Now that we have a **shuffle** function, we can write the function that fills up the table. The function is on the next page.

What happens here is that we go through all the possible options for the image sprite and we select **rows*cols/2** of them to be used in the table with a known sample selection algorithm. For each selected option we need to place two tiles with that option in the table. Again, we think it's it easier for this algorithm to work with a linear table and compute the row and the column once we know what value needs to be stored in the cell.

```
public function fillTable(rows:int, cols:int,
                          options:int)
{
    var k = rows*cols/2;
    var n = options;
    var i = 0, opt = 0;
    while (k > 0) {
        var r = Math.floor(Math.random() *
                          (1+n));
        if (r <= k)
        {
            table[int(i/cols)][i%cols] = opt;
            table[int((i+1)/cols)][(i+1)%cols]
                = opt;
            i+= 2;
            k--;
        }
        opt++;
        n--;
    }
    shuffle(rows, cols);
}
```

Finally, if you want to test out this part (and you should), here's a class function that can be useful:

```
public function traceTable(rows, cols)
{
    for (var i = 0; i<rows; i++)
    {
        for (var j = 0; j<cols; j++)
        {
            trace(i, j, table[i][j]);
        }
    }
}
```

The "trace" function prints the parameters it receives to the Output tab in Flash. It does not affect the execution of the app, but it's useful for debugging.

With this phase accomplished, it's time to write a constructor for the class. It seems necessary to pass the number of rows and columns to the constructor, but also to store them in class variables for later use. Let's add two variables in the class called sizeR and sizeC (or use more creative names if you want). This constructor must initialize the array of arrays that will store the table, then call the function fillTable. We can assume right now that the constructor will need to initialize the tile objects and keep links to them, in which case it will need a reference to the stage that it can pass to the tiles.

```
public function Table(rows:int, cols:int,
                      theStage)
{
    table = new Array(rows);
    for (var i = 0; i<rows; i++)
    {
        table[i] = new Array(cols);
    }
    fillTable(rows, cols, 15);
    sizeR = rows;
    sizeC = cols;
    parent = theStage;
}
```

Before going to the next step, it might be a good idea to test this all out in the project file.

Let's proceed to creating the tile objects and displaying them. We'll need another array created the exact same way as the table. Let's call it "tiles" and add it to the class. First, let's assume that we'll leave some space in the stage above the matrix of tiles for buttons and textual information. It would be useful to store it in a class variable. Declare it as "headspace" and initialize it in the constructor to whatever might be appropriate for you. You can make a guess now and adjust this value later by testing it.

Then start a new function called createTiles with no parameters and allocate the arrays for the tiles with a similar method to the one used for the table. Instead of the parameter "rows" you'll have to use sizeR this time, and instead of "cols", sizeC. Then inside the for loop, after initializing the array for the row i, let's add a loop that creates all the tiles for that row and places them in the appropriate position ("this" identifies the Table object that the function will apply to):

```
for (var j = 0; j<sizeC; j++)
{
    tiles[i][j] = new Tile(parent,
                           table[i][j]);
    tiles[i][j].setPosition(i, j, this);
    tiles[i][j].place(100*j, headspace+100*i);
    tiles[i][j].showBack();
}
```

Note that you have to replace the "100" by whatever size your tiles are. Add a call to this function in the constructor at the end.

The last step for now is to go back to the project file and test this. Add a line at the top importing the **Table** file. Then comment out the creation of the single tile by adding two forward slashes "//" at the beginning of every line to be commented out. Then declare an object of type **Table** and with the parameters for the row and column having the values you chose for your table in the game, and **this.stage** passed in the third place for the parameter **theStage**.

Note that the keyword "**this**" represents the object in the app that the code applies to. In the context of a class, it will be the object of that class that a class method is called from, known in object oriented programming as the *target object*. In the context of code added to the Actions panel of some entity, **this** identifies that entity. In the case above, **this** represents the frame of the application inside which the code will run. If we had written the code in the Actions panel of a button, then **this** would represent the button itself. You can think of it as the *owner* of the code.

If everything went well and there are no errors, now you should see the whole setup of tiles, and when you click on any of them, they should show the image randomly chosen for them. You can verify that you have indeed the right tiles in a random order. When you run the program again, a different configuration of images should appear. You can tweak the position of the tiles at this point to make sure that they are well centered.

Core Game Functionality

Now that we have the basic mechanics of the classes down, it's time to string it all together and make the game work.

We need a class variable in the class **Table** to indicate if a tile that was clicked is the first one in the guessing process or the second. We'll also need the position of the previously clicked tile with row and column. Let's declare 3 variables, **first**, **prevR, prevC**. The first one can be declared as a **Boolean** (taking the values **true/false**) and the two others as **int**:

```
var first:Boolean;
```

Before doing anything else, initialize this variable to **true** in the function **createTiles**. It is better to do it in this function because if we want to play the game again without restarting the app, this function will be called instead of the constructor.

Next we'll declare a function in the class **Table** that the tile can call when it is clicked. It will need to pass to the table its row and column. The case where the first tile is clicked is easy. We just need to set the value of the three new variables appropriately. When the second tile is clicked, we need to check if it matches the first one. If it does, we must leave them both open - but we still have to change the color of the frame. If it doesn't, we need to close them both. The function is at the top of the next page.

Then this function needs to be called. Go back to the **Tile** class and add this line to the function **clickOpen**:

```
theTable.clickTile(row, col);
```

You can test the program now and it should pretty much be working. Note that the second tile is closing too fast to see what it is. To make it stay open a while longer, we need to introduce a **Timer**.

```
public function clickTile(row:int, col:int)
{
    if (first)
    {
        prevR = row;
        prevC = col;
        first = false;
    }
    else
    {
        first = true;
        if (table[row][col] ==
            table[prevR][prevC])
        {
            tiles[row][col].showFound();
            tiles[prevR][prevC].showFound();
        }
        else
        {
            tiles[row][col].showBack();
            tiles[prevR][prevC].showBack();
        }
    }
}
```

Timer

Timer is a class that allows us to do something repeatedly at specific intervals, and it's also the only way to delay something in Flash (or at least that we know of). We'll only need to declare one timer object in the **Table** class for this, and then start it and stop it as needed.

Before we do that, though, we have to declare two more variables in the class for the row and column of the clicked tiles. Since the function **clickTile** will not close the tiles itself but only start the timer, and the timer function doesn't allow for extra parameters to be passed to it, we'll store this information in the class variables. We already know the row and column of the first tile. We also need to store those of the second tile.

Let's call them **secondR** and **secondC**.

Now let's add the function to be called after a given amount of time (to be determined):

```
public function closeTiles(event:TimerEvent)
{
    tiles[secondR][secondC].showBack();
    tiles[prevR][prevC].showBack();
}
```

Then replace the two lines that close the tiles in the function **clickTile** with an assignment of **row** and **col** to the variables **secondR** and **secondC**.

Go back to the beginning of the class and declare a new variable called **tileTimer** with the type **Timer**. In the constructor we need to initialize the timer with a parameter representing the delay in milliseconds, and attach a function to this timer to be called when it is activated. This can be done like this:

```
tileTimer = new Timer(700);
tileTimer.addEventListener(TimerEvent.TIMER,
                           closeTiles);
```

You can adjust the delay when you test the program.

What is left to do is to start and stop this timer. The timer needs to be started in the function **clickTile** after the variables **secondR** and **secondC** have been assigned their values:

```
tileTimer.start();
```

The timer needs to be stopped inside its own function **closeTiles**, after the whole content of its body:

```
tileTimer.stop();
```

Test the game to make sure it's working. We can now focus on some GUI details next to complete the application.

Button

Let's add a button at the top that can be used to restart the game. Go back to the project file. From the Window menu open Components. Drag a button from the dialog to the stage and place it in the middle above the area of the tiles. From the Window menu again, open the Component Inspector dialog and make sure that the button is selected. Click on the first tab called Parameters and change its label to **Restart**. Then in the Properties area, find Color Effects, change it from None to Tint, and then choose the color that you want for the button. Finally, at the top of the Properties area, you'll see something called Instance Name. Edit that field and give it the name **startButton**. This is a unique identifier for the button that will allow us to manipulate it in the code.

Let's go back to the **Tile** class and add a function that restarts the game without re-building the tiles. All we need to change in this case is the image sprite. First we have to remove it from the stage and hide it, and then we can replace it with a new one:

```
public function replay(option)
{
    var posx = imageSprite.x;
    var posy = imageSprite.y;
    imageSprite.visible = false;
    parent.removeChild(imageSprite);
    chooseBmp(option);
    moveTo(imageSprite, posx, posy);
    imageSprite.visible = false;
}
```

With this function written, we can write another one in the class

Table with the same purpose. This function will be somewhat similar to the constructor, so we can add it right after it, but many operations don't need to be redone, like the array allocation. The last line in the function **replay** is a call to the garbage collector that hopefully will recycle the memory used by the image sprites that we have disposed of.

```
public function replay()
{
    fillTable(sizeR, sizeC, 15);
    for (var i = 0; i < sizeR; i++)
    {
        for (var j = 0; j < sizeC; j++)
        {
            tiles[i][j].replay(table[i][j]);
            tiles[i][j].showBack();
        }
    }
    System.gc();
}
```

The functionality of restarting the game is now ready. Let's go back to the project file and open the Actions dialog. We'll add one function here that will restart the game when called that we can attach to the button. Note that if the code doesn't show up when you switch to the project file, you have to click on Layer 1: Frame 1 in the Actions dialog.

Winning The Game

Usually when the player wins a game, something should happen to mark it out. You can refine this later any way you want (a timed animation can help) but for now let's just make a short and sweet message pop up over the tiles when the game is won. But first we need to figure out when that happens.

In the class **Table**, add a variable called **tileCount** and initialize it in the constructor as **rows*cols/2**. Then in the function **clickTile**, in the case where the tiles match, decrease this variable by 1 (like, **countTile--;** for example).

Go back to the project file. In the stage, add a text area using the tool labeled T, place it in the top center of the screen and type a winning message in it ("you win", "well done", "!!!", etc.). Make the type of the text "Dynamic Text" in the properties. Adjust its size, font, and color; it should be fairly big and visible. When you're happy with it, right-click on the text and choose Convert to Symbol. Give it a symbol name easy to identify and a class name that you can remember. Once you close that dialog, write down the coordinates X and Y of the object on the stage. After that you can delete it from the stage. Click on the Library button (to the left of the properties area) and make sure the symbol you created is there. The whole operation allows us to create a class using vector drawing tools, and use it programmatically in the code at a later time.

In the **Table** class, add another variable called **wonText**. Go back to the function **clickTile**. Here we'll add a test after decreasing the variable **countTile** that will check if the counter is 0. In that case we want to create an instance of the class just defined and place it at the position you wrote down. For example, for me this class is called **WinText**, so the code will look this way: **countTile--;**

```
if (countTile == 0)
{
    wonText = new WinText();
    parent.addChild(wonText);
    wonText.x = 130;
    wonText.y = 160;
}
```

What is left to do is to remove this symbol when the game is restarted. Let's go to the function **replay** in the **Table** class. Add the following lines before the call to the garbage collector:

```
wonText.visible = false;
parent.removeChild(wonText);
wonText = null;
```

Test the program to see that it is working properly.

Sound

The last step in the program will be to add some sound effects to it. The first one will be a small sound that should be heard whenever a tile is clicked. The second one will be a cheering sound for when the game is won. Let's assume that the names of the two sound file we'll be using are **tap.mp3** and **cheer.mp3**. Whichever way you acquire these sound files, save them in the same folder as the rest of the game.

In the project file, go the File menu, and find Import - To Library. Select the mp3 files you created before. Then open the library, right-click on their names, and choose Properties. Check the button Export for ActionScript and give each of them a class name that you can remember. Let us suppose that the classes are called **CheerSound** and **TapSound**.

In the **Table** class we need two variables to reference these sounds; let's call them **tap** and **cheer**. Declare them at the top, and then add these lines to the constructor to define them.

```
tap = new TapSound();
cheer = new CheerSound();
```

Go to the function **clickTile** in the same class and add

```
tap.play();
```

at the beginning. Then in the same function, down inside the test for **countTiles** being 0, add

```
cheer.play();
```

This function is simply playing the sound, as its name indicates. It is not a sophisticated function, because the sound played this way cannot be adjusted for volume, and cannot be interrupted. For the purpose of this game, though, it is sufficient. More elaborate Flash classes can be used for more complex sound manipulation.

On Your Own

Here are a couple of suggestions for things to add on your own:

- make the tap sound different when the tiles match;

- add a little button at the top to turn the sound on and off;

- prevent the user from clicking several tiles in a row before the timer function can turn them off.

The 2D Games Journey

4.3 Select Multiple Objects

For games in this category, the main action in the game requires two or more objects. They need to be identified and stored between user actions. A general schema of the main loop of the game can be seen in Figure 7.

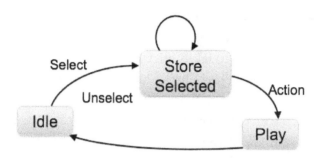

Figure 7. General schema for select multiple objects games

Some examples of games that this description applies to are some of the object matching games involving multiple selections, as for example, puzzles requiring to find 3 or more numbered tiles on a table such that their sum is equal to a given number. Other examples would be token moving games such as chess, in the situations where a move may result in the capture of an adversary piece that needs to be selected from a set of potential candidates.

For these games, the player must select several objects first, and then perform an action. Thus, a game manager, as for example a table, will need to keep references to all the active objects in the game. If the behavior of the tokens is complex enough, they can be implemented as external objects. An additional data structure will have to be created to store selection references. It is possible to simply add an attribute to the class representing the game token to mark them as selected, but without a this data structure added for this purpose, finalizing an action would require an exhaustive traversal of all the game tokens to check for the active ones. This data structure can be a linked list or an array with a counter for the number of stored items.

As an example of such a game we will see next a new tutorial for implementing a game of Yahtzee. Although this game is fairly popular, let us briefly describe it first. The player has a set of 5 dice at his or her disposal and a number of rounds in which to play them. There are a number of combinations available, each of them worth a given number of points, and in each round the player must try and obtain one of the combinations, a different one each time. In each round, the player first rolls all the dice. He or she then has two more attempts where they select any number of the dice to roll again, keeping those that they deem fit for one of the combinations still available to play. After the two sessions of rolling some of the dice again, the player must choose the combination that they want the result to be scored for. If the numbers don't fit the combination, a score of 0 is assigned. Otherwise each successful combination achieved has its own scoring rules. Table 1 shows all possible combinations along with their score.

The goal of the game is to obtain the highest score. If multiple players are involved, they take turns rolling the dice 3 times and scoring a combination, and the player with the highest total score wins.

Table 1. Yahtzee combinations and score

Combination	Score	Description
Ones	Sum of 1s ...	As many dices of 1 as possible; the score adds them up.
Sixes	Sum of 6s	As many dices of 6 as possible; the score adds them up.
Upper bonus	35	If the total score of the number combinations is at least 63.
3 of a kind	Sum	At least 3 dices of any number; the score is the sum of the identical dice.
4 of a kind	Sum	At least 4 dices of any number; the score is the sum of the identical dice.
Full house	25	2 of a number and 3 of another
Small straight	30	4 dices forming a sequence
Large straight	40	5 dices forming a sequence
Yahtzee	50	5 identical dices
Chance	Simple sum	The score adds up all the dices.
Yahtzee bonus	100	Second Yahtzee scored as anything else

Before we start implementing the game, let's discuss its organization. First, the game will have to implement 5 dice that can be rolled, or otherwise said, assigned a random value between 1 and 6. Since there are several complex operations to perform on these dice, it is better to create a class called `Dice` handling them. A second class will manage all of the dice, check for combinations, handle the display, and roll the dice again. We will call this class `Game`. This class will store references to the `Dice` objects in a simple array, and score points in another array.

For the game interactive objects, each die will need a sprite for each possible number it may have to display, as well as a gray one for the dice that are marked to be rolled again. Thus, the `Dice` object will have an attribute called `state` with values in the range 0 to 6; 0 will designate the gray dice that can be rolled. All of these sprites will need to react to mouse events and then send a message to the object of the class `Game`, which means that the `Dice` objects will need to store a reference to it.

The cell displaying each combination in the scoring table will need to react to mouse events such that the player can choose it to be scored. They will also need to store information about the combination that they represent, whether or not it has been used in the game, and the score for it. Displaying the used combinations in a dimmed color might be a good idea, as well as making them not react to mouse events anymore. All this behavior is complex enough to create another class to handle it, that we'll call `ScoreCell`. The class `Game` will store an array of these objects.

We will also need one button for rolling the dice again and for restarting the game.

This game fits the description of a select multiple objects

game for the obvious reason that in order to roll some of the dice again, they must be selected first. The data structure storing the selections here will be the array of **Dice** objects.

Tutorial 3

This tutorial presents the step by step implementation of the Yahtzee game.

Preparation

Let us start by setting up the resources. You'll need a collection of images: one for each face of the dice, and one for a gray die that can be rolled. Create these images with whatever program you want, then save them to the project folder. Figure 8 shows an example of the seven images that we'll be using in this program:

Figure 8. Images used in a Yahtzee game

Project

Create an ActionScript 3 project. The stage area will have to contain on the left side a table that looks like the one shown in Table 2.

On the right hand side of the stage there should be some space for displaying the dice. If you plan on implementing some animation on the rolling dice (optional), then this space should be larger. Below or above the dice space, we'll add a button later for the roll action. The score categories in the table will be created using buttons, to make it easier for the player to choose them.

Table 2. The score board

Combination	Score
Ones	
Twos	
Threes	
Fours	
Fives	
Sixes	
Upper bonus	
3 of a kind	
4 of a kind	
Full house	
Small straight	
Large straight	
Yahtzee	
Chance	
Yahtzee bonus	
Total	

Import images

Import your seven images to the library one by one. For each of them, go to File - Import - To Library, and then select the image form the project folder. Once all the images are in, go to the Library tab next to Properties, right-click on one of the images, and select Properties. Check Export to ActionScript, and underneath, give it a class name you can remember. From here on I'll assume that the names of these classes are `OneBmp` through `SixBmp` and `GrayBmp`. Then click Ok. Now these seven classes should be usable in the code to create objects based on these images.

Score Cell

The score board will be organized in cells, each of them being an object of a class called `ScoreCell`. For this class, we will combine vector drawing techniques in Flash with coding.

Let's start by creating one row of the table score using Flash's vector drawing. You need one rectangle for the name of the combination, and a smaller one next to it for the score of that combination. Then on top of the first rectangle, add a text box and write the text **Large Straight** inside, since this is likely to be the longest combination name on the board. Adjust the font, size and colors the way you prefer. On top of the score box, add another text box in a similar font and size, and write the text 40 inside. The objects might look like in the following image shown in Figure 9.

Figure 9. One cell of the score board

Then write down on a piece of paper the coordinates of each of the four objects (two boxes, two text boxes) as well as the coordinates and dimensions of the background box.

Move the text boxes away from the rectangles they are shown on. This is to make other operations on these objects easier. Use the selection tool to select the entire first rectangle along with its borders. For this, select an area around it instead of clicking on it, because Flash treats the borders of the rectangle as separate objects. Then group the rectangle and its borders, and convert it to a symbol. Name the symbol **Box1** and export it for ActionScript. Repeat the operation with the second rectangle, and call the class **Box2**.

Class

Create a new ActionScript file of type class under the name **ScoreCell**. Add the following import statements at the top of the package:

```
import flash.text.TextField;
import flash.display.BitmapData;
import flash.display.Sprite;
import flash.display.Stage;
import flash.events.MouseEvent;
```

Let's start with the class constructor. Just like in the other applications, this class will need a reference to the stage in order to add objects to it dynamically. It will also need values for the top right corner of the position of this cell on the stage, as well as an identifier for the type of combination that the cell represents. To anticipate storing all this information in the class, declare the following class attributes before the constructor: **parent, posX, posY, combination**. Then add the following variables to the constructor: **theStage, origX, origY, option**. Then start the code of the constructor by assigning to each class variable, the value of the corresponding parameter respectively, in this order.

Let's add two boxes using the classes **Box1** and **Box2** that we created by converting the vector drawing objects to symbols. Add the class attributes **boxName**, **boxScore**, **textName**, **textScore** that will store references to the two boxes and the two text fields. Add the following function to the class, after the constructor:

```
function moveTo(spriteObj, valx, valy)
{
    spriteObj.x = valx;
    spriteObj.y = valy;
}
```

To create the first box, we have to create the object itself first, add it to the stage so that it becomes visible and active, and then move it to the correct position on the stage. To summarize this, here is the code:

```
boxName = new Box1;
parent.addChild(boxName);
moveTo(boxName, posX, posY);
```

Add similar code to create the **boxScore**, with the exception that the horizontal position should be shifted forward by a quantity such that the second box is displayed to the right of the first one. The easier way to do this is to go back to the paper where you wrote the coordinates of the two boxes in the original design. Subtract the **x** coordinate of the first box from the **x** coordinate of the second one. The quantity you obtain should be added to **posX** in the **moveTo** function call for the **boxScore**.

Next we'll create a text box for the name of the combination and one for the score. To create the first one, add the following code to the constructor:

```
textName = new TextField();
moveTo(textName, posX+14, posY+6);
textName.width = 200;
textName.text = "Small Straight";
parent.addChild(textName);
```

Replace 14 and 6 with numbers computed based on the difference between the values of **X** and **Y** of the score box and of the rectangle behind it in the original layout you drew. Replace the 200 for the width with the width of your text box (that you have written down). Then do something similar for the **textScore**. Testing the app, you'll see that the text is in the right position, but most likely, is not in the right font. Back at the top of the package, import the module **flash.text.TextFormat**. After the text boxes are created, let's create an object of type **TextFormat** to define their attributes. Add the class attribute **txtFormat** in case we need to use it again when we set the score dynamically during the execution of the game. Go back to the stage first and write down the name of the font and its size. While you're there, click on either of the text boxes, then on the button Embed next to the font name in the Properties area. Select all the uppercase and lowercase letters, as well as the numerals (or digits), then click OK. Then go back to the **ScoreCell** class and add the following code before the definition of the text boxes:

```
txtFormat = new TextFormat;
txtFormat.font = "Arial Rounded MT Bold";
txtFormat.size = 18;
```

Replace the name of the font in quotes with the name of the font that you've chosen. Then add the following line right after the text of the **textName** box has been defined, and then a similar one for the **textScore**:

```
textName.setTextFormat(txtFormat);
```

To test this class and make sure that it works so far, go back to the game project and add the following lines to the Actions window:

```
import ScoreCell;
var cell = new ScoreCell(this.stage,
                         200, 20, 1);
```

Next, let's add a function to the class that sets the text of the cell with the right value based on the **option** attribute of the object. Normally the indexes in an array start from 0, which would mean that the first combination, the Ones, would correspond to an option value of 0. To keep things simpler, we'll choose to have the values of the options starting from 1 instead of 0, so that the first six combinations are easier to score. First, add a class variable called "score" and one called "used". The purpose of the second one is to mark the fact that the combination in this cell has been used already and not let it be scored again. We cannot just use the score to determine if a combination has been used or not because a score of 0 is possible in the game. Assign values of 0 and **false** respectively to these variables in the constructor. Add the following function after the constructor:

```
function setCombination()
{
    var names = ["", "Ones", "Twos"];
    textName.text = names[combination];
}
```
Then complete the rest of the array names with all of the other combinations. This creates a C-style array containing the names, and we can extract the one that is appropriate for the

combination that applies to that particular **ScoreCell** object. The first element of this array is an empty string because we don't use the combination number 0. Replace the instruction setting the text of the **textName** with a function call to this function.

Test this class as it is at this point to make sure everything works. After that you can delete the vector drawing objects in the stage. In the next part we'll start working on the **Game** class.

The Game Class

Start a new ActionScript class file and call it **Game**. Import the module **ScoreCell** in this class.

Declare a class attribute called **scoreArray** and one called **parent**. In the constructor, add the same parameter for the stage as in the class **ScoreCell** and initialize the **parent** attribute the same way. Next, we'll need to create the table of score cells. These will need to store a reference to the **Game** object to send it information about being selected for scoring. Thus, go back to the **ScoreCell** class and add a parameter in the constructor after the stage called **gameVal**. Add a class attribute called **gameRef** and then initialize it with the value of the parameter in the constructor.

Back in the class **Game**, initialize the array of score cells with the following code. First, we create the array itself. Second, we use a loop to initialize each score cell object in the array. Add **combNum** as a class attribute.

```
combNum = 17;
scoreArray = new Array(combNum);
for (var i = 1; i<combNum; i++)
{
```

```
    scoreArray[i] = new ScoreCell(parent, this,
                          20, 35*i-15, i);
}
```

In this piece of code, the **x** coordinate of the score cells is a constant because they are supposed to be aligned vertically. The **y** coordinate is computed based on the value of the variable **i**, and on the height of the box objects that you wrote down at the beginning, plus a couple of pixels for padding. You will have to use values based on the size of your own box, and may have to adjust the size of the stage to make sure all the cells fit in.

To test this code, go back to the **yahtzee.fla** project file and replace the code testing a single cell with the following:

```
var gameRef = new Game(this.stage);
```

As we now have a better idea about how the largest object will fit on the stage, it's time to add some buttons for the game functionality. Add two buttons to the stage and edit their labels in the Properties section to show **New Game** and **Roll** respectively. You can find the button component in the Components menu situated between the Properties area and the stage. Give them instance names **newGameBtn** and **rollBtn**. Their size and placement is up to you.

Let's implement the functionality of a new game. First, go to the **ScoreCell** class and add a public function called **reset**. In this function, set the **text** of the **textScore** as an empty string (" "), the value of the attribute **score** to 0, and the value of the attribute **used** to **false**. While you're doing this, also set the **text** of the **textScore** attribute in the constructor as an empty string. The value we've used before was only for testing.

Next, go back to the class **Game** and add the following function:

```
public function newGame()
{
    for (var i = 1; i<combNum; i++)
    {
        scoreArray[i].reset();
    }
}
```

Then go to the **yahtzee.fla** project file and add the following code:

```
newGameBtn.addEventListener(MouseEvent.CLICK,
                            restart);
function restart(event)
{
    gameRef.newGame();
}
```

To test the functionality of this button, you can temporarily use some random text in the function **reset** in the class **ScoreCell** instead of an empty string. Once you see it appear in the cells when running the app, you can erase it and revert to an empty string.

While working on the **ScoreCell** class, we can add another function that will be useful later, that sets the text of the score for the object. It is necessary to set the format of the text field again after we give the text a new value, because otherwise it will revert to the default format.

```
public function setScore(val)
{
    score = val;
    textScore.text = score;
    textScore.setTextFormat(txtFormat);
```

}

Next we'll define the `Dice` class.

The Dice Class

Create a new ActionScript class file and call it `Dice.as`. Copy the function `moveTo` from the class `ScoreCell` into this one. Then add the following function that is very similar to some functions seen in the previous tutorials. You'll have to import the modules

```
flash.display.BitmapData,
flash.display.Sprite,
flash.geom.Matrix.
```

```
public function makeSprite(bmpName, bmpSize,
                                 spriteSize)
{
    var sprite = new Sprite();
    var factor = 1.0*spriteSize;
    factor / =  bmpSize;
    var sclMatrix = new Matrix();
    sclMatrix.identity();
    sclMatrix.scale(factor, factor);
    sprite.graphics.beginBitmapFill(bmpName,
                                       sclMatrix);
    sprite.graphics.drawRect(0, 0, spriteSize,
                               spriteSize);
    sprite.graphics.endFill();
    return sprite;
}
```

Declare the class attributes **parent** and **gameRef** just like in the class `ScoreCell`. Then add the corresponding parameters to the constructor and initialize them the same way. Then in the constructor for the class **Dice**, add two more parameters for the position x and y. Declare the class attributes **posX, posY** and initialize them with the values of these parameters.

In the constructor we need to initialize all the sprites used by the **Dice** object. Unlike the score cells that display a single combination name through the game, the content of each die is dynamic, and changes randomly every time the die is rolled. Thus, each **Dice** object will need to store a sprite for each of the seven images. The easiest way to handle this is to store them in an array. To begin with, declare the class attributes sprites and **spriteNum**, and then add the following code to the constructor:

```
spriteNum = 7;
var bmp = new Array(spriteNum);
sprites = new Array(spriteNum);
bmp = new GrayBmp(84, 84);
sprites[0] = makeSprite(bmp, 84, 80);
parent.addChild(sprites[0]);
moveTo(sprites[0], posX, posY);
```

This code is similar to what we have seen in the other tutorials: we need to create a bitmap using the class created by importing the image, create the sprite from it, add it to the stage to make it visible, and then move it to the right position. Replace the number 84 by the size of the dice image you are using and the number 80 with the size that you want to display the dice on the screen with.

Before adding all the other sprites, let's test this one and create the five dice that will be part of the game. For this, in the **Game** class import the **Dice** class at the top. Then in the constructor add the following code:

```
var d = new Dice(parent, this, 352, 150);
```

Adjust the numbers 352 and 150 such that the die appears in a convenient position on the stage.

Once this part is working, let's add the five dice to the **Game** class. Declare a class attribute called **diceArray** and initialize it in the constructor as an array of five elements. Use a **for** loop (starting from 0 this time) after that to assign to each of these elements a new object of type **Dice**. Use the initialization of the **ScoreCell** array as a model for the parameters in each of these function calls. Also use a class attribute called **diceNum** to store the number of dice (5), so as not to use the constant 5 everywhere.

Once this is working, go back to the constructor for the class **Dice** and add all the images as sprites. First, you'll have to add the bitmaps one by one because the classes defining them cannot be stored in an array. Then turn the rest of the sprite-defining code into a **for** loop. Add the following line to hide these sprites:

```
sprites[i].visible = false;
```

Then after the loop, make **sprites[0]** visible again.

We will need an attribute to keep track of the number displayed on the die, and at the same time, the active visible sprite. Declare this attribute with the name **number** and initialize it in the constructor.

Set Sprite

Let's write a function in the **Dice** class that assigns a new number to the die object and sets the appropriate sprite as visible. This function will take a new number as parameter. What we have to do is make the currently active sprite invisible, set the new one as visible, and store its number in the class attribute. Here is this function:

```
public function setSprite(option)
{
    sprites[number].visible = false;
    sprites[option].visible = true;
    number = option;
}
```

Roll the Dice

Now would be a good time to write a function that rolls the die. What we need in this function is to generate a random number between 1 and 6, and then to call the previous function to set the sprite. First, import the module **Math**. This module contains a function called **random** that generates a random number between 0 and 1, not including 1. To turn it into an integer between 1 and 6, we need to multiply it by 6, convert to an integer, and then add 1 to the result. Add the following function to the class **Dice**:

```
public function roll()
{
    var r = 1 + int(Math.random() *
                    (spriteNum-1));
    setSprite(r);
}
```

Now we can add a similar function to the class **Game** that rolls all the dice:

```
public function roll()
{
    for (var i = 0; i<diceNum; i++)
    {
        diceArray[i].roll();
    }
}
```

To test this function, in the **yahtzee.fla** project file, add a call to it from the **gameRef** object after the objects are created. Once it works, turn it into a function called **rollDice** in frame 1, and then attach it as a callback for a mouse up event on the button **rollBtn**. Now the roll button should show a new combination of dice every time it is clicked.

To take us one step closer to the game functionality, in the function **roll** in the class **Dice**, add a test for the **number** attribute being 0 before the operations are done. After this, the roll button should function only the first time you click it.

Another easy step is to make the function **newGame** also reset the dice. For this, add a line ion the body of this function consisting of a function call to **setSprite(0)** originating from each of the five dice. You'll need a **for** loop for it. Then the **newGame** button will reset all the dice to gray, and the roll button will generate new random numbers for them.

Dice Events

After all the dice are rolled, there are two rounds where the player can click on them to select those he or she wants to roll again. Thus, we need to attach a mouse event to all the number sprites such that when we click on them, they become gray. If we want to implement the game correctly, we have to allow the player to unselect a die for re-roll and go back to the number it displayed before it was selected. For this, a class attribute will have to store this number. Declare the attribute **lastNum** in the class **Dice** and initialize it as 0 in the constructor.

We need to plan for one more thing before setting up these events. After the second time that the player has rolled the dice again, they should select a scoring combination. The game should not allow them at that point to select dice to roll again. For this, we can add an attribute to the class **Dice** to store a flag that can be turned on when the last roll has happened and prevent the dice form reacting to the mouse. Let's declare an attribute called **lastRoll** in this class and initialize it as **false** in the constructor. Then go back to the function **roll** and add the following parameter:

```
roll(isLastRoll = false)
```

This will give it a default value of **false** in case it is absent form the function call. Then before the end of the function, assign the value of this parameter to the variable **lastRoll**.

Add the following function to the class **Dice**. Basically if the **lastRoll** flag is not up, then if the current number on the die is 0, we revert the die to the previously displayed number. Otherwise we set the value of the **lastNum** to the current one, and then set the die to gray, which is the sprite 0.

```
public function selectDie(event:MouseEvent)
{
    if (!lastRoll)
    {
        if (number == 0 && lastNum ! =  0)
        {
            setSprite(lastNum);
        }

        else
        {
            lastNum = number;
            setSprite(0);
        }
    }
```

}

To attach this function as an event to the sprite, go back to the constructor, and add the following line inside the `for` loop where the sprites are created, after the line adding the sprite as a child to the parent.

```
sprites[i].addEventListener(MouseEvent.CLICK,
                          selectDie);
```

Test the app to see if this functionality works. After rolling the dice, you should be able to click on each of them to turn them gray (or select them for re-roll), and then click on them again to restore the number they were showing before.

One last thing that we can do in the class **Dice** is to turn the **number** attribute into a public one. We must do this because the number will have to be accessed from the **Game** class. By default, attributes are private, meaning that we can only access them inside the class. So remove the declaration of this attribute from where it is right now, and add another line for it:

```
public var number;
```

In the last part of this tutorial we'll implement the functionality of the game.

Core Game Functionality

We have created all the classes involved in the game, have set up the stage, and placed all the objects on it. We can now start to work towards the game functionality.

The first part we can focus on is the functionality of the rolls. For every combination, the dice are first rolled, then the player selects some of them, and then they are rolled again. This will have to be implemented in the class **Game**. Add two class attributes to this class called **rollNum** and **scored**. Initialize them both to 0 in the constructor.

Modify the function **roll** the following way: after the loop, increment the value of the variable **rollNum**. Then place the function call to the function **roll** for each die inside a conditional, where you test if the roll number is less than 2, and if it is, perform the call as it is, otherwise call the function **roll** with a parameter of value **true**. Place the entire body of the function inside a conditional testing if **rollNum** is less than 3.

Run the app to test this new functionality.

Next, we can organize the rolls and re-rolls at the level of the class **Game**. In the function **roll** in this class, that is called by clicking the **Roll** button, we should allow the dice to be rolled only when the current number of rolls doesn't exceed 2. The scoring function will reset the number of rolls to 0. We'll assume that the first roll happens automatically, and then the player will be able to do it manually twice. After each roll, we'll increase the value of the variable **rollNum**. All we have to do is to place the entire code of the function **roll** inside the following conditional and add a statement incrementing this variable:

```
if (rollNum < 3)
{
    rollNum++;
```
Once this is working, add an instruction to the function **newGame** where you reset this variable to 0.

Next, we can focus on the scoring functionality. The scoring itself can be implemented in the class **ScoreCell**, since that is where the mouse event will be directed, but it will need to retrieve the values of all the dice for this purpose. Thus, we need a function in the class **Game** that can deliver these values. Since the dice can form any given combination regardless of the order in which they are, it would make sense for this function to sort these values in ascending order before communicating them to the score cell. This way, the scoring function can assume that these values are in order.

In the class **Game**, add the following function.

```
public function retrieveDice()
{
    var dice = new Array(5);
    for (var i = 0; i<diceNum; i++)
    {
        dice[i] = diceArray[i].number;
    }
    dice.sort();
    return dice;
}
```

In the same class, we'll need a function that can be called once the score is computed to update the interface elements and re-roll the dice. The function is shown next.

```
public function recordScore(scoreVal)
{
    scored++;
    scoreArray[combNum-1].score +=  scoreVal;
    scoreArray[combNum-1].
        setScore(scoreArray[combNum-1].score);
    rollNum = 0;
    for (var i = 0; i<diceNum; i++)
    {
        diceArray[i].setSprite(0);
    }
}
```

Going now to the class **ScoreCell**, since the previous function needs to access the **score** attribute, turn this into a **public** one. Then let's add a function that will be called on a mouse click event:

```
public function scoreMe(event:MouseEvent)
{
    if (!used)
    {
        used = true;
        var dice = gameRef.retrieveDice();
        score = computeScore(dice);
        setScore(score);
        gameRef.recordScore(score);
    }
}
```

To test this function, add a function called **computeScore** taking one parameter and returning a constant. Then go back to the class constructor and add this line at the end to make the name box react to the mouse click, then add a similar one for the second box and for each of the text fields.

```
boxName.addEventListener(MouseEvent.CLICK,
                         scoreMe);
```

At this point you should be able to test the functionality of the app.

There is one more step to do before we can start implementing the scoring: we don't want the **Total** box, the **Upper Bonus** box, and the **Yahtzee Bonus** box to react to mouse clicks, since these are not set by scoring a combination. Thus, place the four statements setting the mouse events in a conditional testing that the attribute **combination** does not have the values 7, 15, or 16.

The last thing to do is to go ahead and actually implement the scoring function. To organize this process, we start with a driver function that will select the type of evaluation to be done based on the combination number. Then this function will call one of a set of functions doing the actual computations. Test each of the scoring functions as soon as you can.

To get started, let's write a function that computes the score for the first six number combinations. To make this function more easily reusable, let's have the number passed in as a parameter. All we have to do here is go through the array of dice numbers and add the ones equal to the target number. This is an adaptation of a simple function "find" or "locate" that is present in many textbooks.

```
public function addTarget(dice, target)
{
    var i, sum = 0;
    for (i = 0; i<5; i++)
    {
        if (dice[i] == target)
        {
            sum += target;
        }
    }
    return sum;
}
```

Replace the statement returning a constant in the function computeScore in the class with the following code. This will be our driver function.

```
if (combination <= 6)
{
    return addTarget(dice, combination);
}
```

The next one to implement would be the **Three of a Kind**, but the same function can also be used for the **Four of a Kind**. Considering that the dice are ordered, we need to check for the longest contiguous sequence of equal dice. We will need two loops for this: one with a variable **j** marking the beginning of the sequence, and a second one with a variable **i**, counting the dice equal to the first one in the sequence. Then if the length of the sequence, computed as the difference between **i** and **j**, is at least equal to the required length, we can return the sum of the dice in the sequence. Otherwise if we don't find such a sequence, we return 0.

Note that we're only going to check if we have such a sequence for those positions where we still have at least **count** following dice. This is why the continuation condition for the loop doesn't simply test that **j** is less than 5. A second remark is that in the **while** loop, we don't increment the variable **j** by one every time. Thus, we can skip all the dice following the position **j** that have the same number as **j**. These cannot be part of the next combination anyway. After the **for** loop, **i** ends up being the position of the first dice with a value different from before, which is where the next sequence will start.

```
public function countOfAKind(dice, count)
{
    var i, j = 0, sum;
    while (j <= 5-count)
    {
        sum = 0;
        for (i=j; i<5 && dice[i]==dice[j]; i++)
        {
            sum +=  dice[j];
        }
        if (i-j >= count)
        {
            return sum;
```

```
        }
        j = i;
    }
    return 0;
}
```

Going back to the function **computeScore**, add the following **else** to the conditional. This contains a **switch** statement that will allow us to add more cases later.

```
else
{
    switch (combination)
    {
        case 8:
        case 9: return countOfAKind(dice,
                        combination - 5);
    }
}
```

Note that in the instructions above, we mean for the function **counfOfAKind** to be called both for the **combination** being equal to 8 and to 9.

We will not detail all of the scoring functions here, but will briefly discuss them. For the full house, a positive score can be returned either if the first three dice are equal to each other and the last two are equal to each other, or the other way around (first two, last three). The small straight and large straight can be implemented under a single function that looks for contiguous sequences of a given length such that each dice in the sequence is one higher than the previous one. This function can be very similar to the function **countOfAKind** above, but special treatment must be done for the duplicate numbers, since they will break the contiguous sequence. A **yahtzee** combination can be tested with a function call to **countOfAKind** with the second parameter having the value 5, except that the return value should be 50 in all the cases and not the value returned by the function **countOfAKind**. The Chance combination is a simple sum of all the dice numbers.

On your own:

- Add some functionality to the game such that if the dice have been re-rolled twice already, then cannot be selected anymore.

- Update the Upper bonus and the Yahtzee bonus after the scoring.

- Change the color of the boxes or of the text for scoring cells that have been used already.

- Detect and mark the game being over, when the last combination has been scored.

5. Animated Game Loops

For all the games where the state changes periodically even without user interaction, as shown in Figure 10.

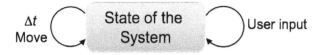

Figure 10. General schema for animated loop games

Here, the *system* is a collection of objects/critters/sprites with behavior defined by rules expressed in the function *move* or *update*. The *state* of the system is the set of values/attributes for each object at a given time. One or more *timers* cause the move functions to be called.

Here are a few elements specific to these games:

- A game object representing the *player's avatar* in the game. The player has control of the movement of this avatar and can activate other actions attached to it, such as jumping or shooting. Exceptions to this feature can be found, such as Tower Defense type of games.
- *Environment objects* such as walls, furniture, floors, and the ground. These objects typically do not interact with the player's avatar directly, but they influence its movement and that of other critters. On one hand, they prevent move through them, defining the space in which the player can physically roam. On the other hand, they determine the vertical coordinate of any critter that is on them. Collision

detection is necessary with these objects when the player is moving.

- *Passive game tokens.* These are objects of type gear or power-up. They cannot be considered part of the environment because the player has a stronger interactive connection with them than with the environment. They are collectable and can provide help with achieving the game objectives. For example, they might restore health or grant special abilities that can give an edge in battle. Collision and proximity detection are necessary with these objects, but the interaction happens only if initiated by the player. In this respect, these objects are similar in functionality to those found in reactive games.

- *Critters* or sprites with independent behavior. These are usually adversaries that the player must dispose of. Their animation is based on a separate timeline than the player's avatar and thus, the best implementation model for them is using an independent timer. For these critters, collision or proximity detection with the player is necessary and usually results in special actions in the game, such as losing a life or engaging in battle. Based on how these critters are created, we can distinguish
  o spontaneously spawning critters, that the game itself creates for the players, such as the PacMan ghosts,
  o player generated critters, that appear in the game as a result of some action from the player, such as bullets.

The game is mostly defined by the collection of all of these elements, and by their interaction with the player and with each other. They are also present in three dimensional animated games, being different mostly in terms of complexity. We will discuss some examples of games where several of these elements are present further in this chapter.

5.1 Timing in a Game

There are several measures that define the timing in a game.

The number of *Frames Per Second* (FPS) is the number of times per second that the graphics display is updated. This measure depends on the platform and on the game demand and settings in terms of resources.

The number of *Cycles Per Second* (CPS) is the number of times per second that the game updates itself.

The physics engine *time step* is a constant (Δt) representing the lapse of time used by the physics engine in the game to compute the next state of the game.

Traditionally, we can see the following elements in a generic game loop:

```
gameLoop() {
    while (not exit) {
        for (1/(cps * dt) times)
            physics.update();
        update_userInput();
        for (all the characters in the game)
            character.move();
        checkSolveInteractions();
        redisplay();
        playSounds();
        restartTimer(1/cps);
    }
}
```

The highest update frequency is most likely that of the physics engine, as this is the part of the game that requires the most precise computations. This is computed as $1/\Delta t$. The next one typically is the FPS for arcade games, while the smallest number is the CPS. This is because in two dimensional games, changes in the game are usually reflected right away in changes on the screen. In a 3D game things could conceivably be different, especially in multi-player games.

5.2 Character Interaction and Collision Detection

The first step in the character interaction is identifying all the game objects that may interact. This step depends largely on the world representation, as discussed in Chapter 2. It is also a deciding factor in choosing the world representation.

The second step consists of testing if any two objects selected for interaction are close enough for that interaction to happen. This is usually done through *collision detection*. This is one of the most complex problems in games programming. The complexity of this operation also depends on the world representation.

For implicit worlds, each object in the game must be tested for collision with all the other objects that can influence its movement, even inactive ones like the walls. For explicit or zone-based worlds, an object can limit its interaction to the objects in its vicinity. This can significantly reduce the computation time, but at the expense of memory use.

The second factor determining the collision computations is the shape of the objects. The problem is relatively easy for simple objects such as spheres or boxes, but it can get complicated really fast for polygons. This is why a common tool used by games is a bounding sphere or box. Often called *collision geometry*, it is an object leading to simpler collision computations that surrounds the object. It is used to filter out many of the potential collisions. Some game or physics engines, like Newton, will provide the tools to define both the collision geometry and the display geometry for each object, the former oftentimes being much simpler than the latter.

Sphere Versus Point

Let's start with the simplest case. A *point P* intersects a *sphere* $S(C, r)$ of center C and radius r if the distance between the point and the center of the sphere is less than or equal to the radius of the sphere.

$d(P, c) \leq r$

Figure 11 shows two examples of points, one of them inside the sphere, and one of them outside of it.

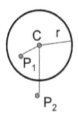

Figure 11. Collision between a point and a sphere: P_1 is inside, P_2 is outside

Sphere Versus Sphere

For the next simplest case, two spheres of $S(C_1, r_1)$ and $S(C_2, r_2)$ of centers C_1 and C_2 and radii r_1 and r_2 respectively intersect if the distance between their centers is less than or equal to the sum of the two radii:

$$d(C_1, C_2) \leq r_1 + r_2$$

Figure 12 shows an example of intersecting spheres.

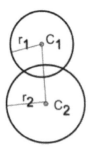

Figure 12. Two intersecting spheres

Box Versus Box

Before we talk about boxes, let's take a look at their one-dimensional versions. Two real *intervals*, $[a, b]$ and $[c, d]$ intersect, if either $a \leq c \leq b$, or $a \leq d \leq b$. Figure 13 shows the two situations described by these inequalities. Note that these formulas still hold even for the case where one interval is completely contained inside the other one.

Figure 13. Intersecting intervals

If the four numbers are given to us without order, such that we don't know whether $a \leq b$ or $b \leq a$, and the same about c and d, we can test the following condition. The four numbers will always satisfy this if the intervals overlap, no matter what order they are in.

$$((c-a)*(c-b) <= 0 || (d-a)*(d-b) <= 0)$$

Moving up in complexity, two boxes oriented along the major axes intersect if their projections intersect in all dimensions. The projection of such a box on one dimension is an interval spanning from its lowest to its highest value of that coordinate. Thus, we can reduce the problem to multiple tests of interval collision detection. Figure 14 illustrates this concept.

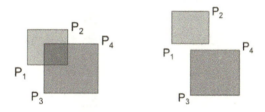

Figure 14. Two intersecting boxes on the left, and non-intersecting on the right

Thus, the 3 dimensional boxes defined by the corners P_1, P_2, and P_3, P_4 respectively present a non empty intersection if

$$[P_1.x, P_2.x] \text{ intersects } [P_3.x, P_4.x] \text{ and}$$

$$[P_1.y, P_2.y] \text{ intersects } [P_3.y, P_4.y] \text{ and}$$

$$[P_1.z, P_2.z] \text{ intersects } [P_3.z, P_4.z] \text{ and}$$

If the boxes are not aligned with the major axes, then the collision is usually handled in two steps. First, a transformation is applied to the objects to make one of the boxes aligned with the major axes. Second, we compute the collision of the aligned

box with the second one, to which the same transformation is applied. If the second box also turns out to be aligned with the major axes, then the method described above is applied. If not, then we can treat the second box as a polygon or a collection of polygons.

Sphere Versus Line

A *line* crosses a *sphere* if the projection point of the center of the sphere on the line is inside the sphere, as shown in Figure 15. The projection point can be obtained by drawing a line through the center of the sphere in a direction perpendicular to the test line. Once we have this point, the problem is reduced to the case described earlier. We'll provide the equations for the 2D case.

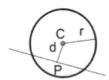

Figure 15. A line crossing a sphere

In the 2D case, a line is determined by the expression $y = mx + a$, with the exception of straight vertical lines. A perpendicular line can be expressed as $y = -1/m\, x + b$, where the constant b can be computed based on the fact that the center C of the sphere is on this line. Then the intersection of the two lines is given by a point $P(x, y)$ that satisfies both equations. This gives us a system of two linear equations in x and y. Solving it will give us the coordinates of the intersection point P. After that, all that is left to do is to compute the distance between the center and this point.

The two exceptions to this method are the horizontal and vertical lines, which are easy to figure out.

Sphere Versus Box

The intersection between a *box* and a *sphere* is a more complicated problem. There are several shortcuts to consider:

- The box has a bounding sphere centered in the intersection of the diagonals and of radius equal to half of the diagonal. If the bounding sphere does not intersect the test sphere, then there is no intersection with the box either.
- The box contains an inner sphere with the center at the diagonal intersection and radius equal to half of the smallest of the sides. If the inner sphere intersects the test sphere, then the box intersects it too.
- If any of the corners of the box is inside the sphere, we have intersection.
- If any of the sides of the box crosses the sphere, then we have intersection.

There are still some situations that are not covered by any of the tests above. A game might want to limit such intersections to either the outer sphere, or the inner sphere, or one in between. In that case, the test will be an approximation, but for the purpose of some games it might still provide enough realism with a reasonable amount of computations.

5.3 A Character-Based Animated Game

In this section we'll discuss a game where the player is in control of an avatar in the game, a sprite whose motion it can control directly. This game will also feature velocity-based movement and other sprites with independent movement or behavior.

The structure of the game is the following:

- We have a character for the player represented by an icon (a ship) that can move in four directions using keyboard interaction.
- There are a number of other objects in the game, some with positive effect on the player, others with negative effect.
- The other objects move on the basis on an initial position and speed; a timer is needed to animate them.
- Collision detection is necessary between the player and the other objects.

Tutorial 4

In this tutorial we'll implement a 2D Shooter game implemented in a Scroller environment. The goal is to control a ship flying through a sky that moves vertically, and to shoot at enemies coming your way. The game will also feature some objects that the player can catch for bonus points.

Resources

Open Flash CS5. As in the previous tutorials, create a new ActionScript 3.0 project. Save the file under a new name. Make sure that the stage has a size of 550x400 (the default size). We will assume that the developing environment is displayed in the

Classic format. If you feel more comfortable working with a different window arrangement, that is fine.

Create two images, one that will serve for a scrolling sky, and one for an aircraft. Since the game will be scrolling vertically, the sky image needs to be vertically circular, meaning that the pixels on the bottom row must be identical or very similar to those on the top row. The easiest way to create such an image is to start from some image of the sky, double its size vertically without resizing (just make a larger canvas), then keeping the original image at the bottom, make a copy on the upper side and reverse it vertically.

The width of the image will eventually match the width of the stage, while the height will be used for the scrolling; thus, the image should be taller than it is wide. Save these images in the same folder as the project. Figure 16 shows an example of the two images (the aircraft is based on a NASA design).

The goal of this part of the tutorial is to make this image continuously scroll in the background. You can also download the second image that we'll use for the plane later. We will accomplish this by storing it in a Sprite object and displaying it at a position that changes with each new frame. There will be some frames where the starting position for the sprite is somewhere in the middle of the screen, which means that it will not cover the stage completely. For those cases, we will have a duplicate of the sprite that can be displayed in such a way that one end of it reaches to the other end of the first sprite, and together they cover the entire visible region of the stage.

Figure 16. The sky and aircraft images

Let us assume that the sky image is called **skyBg.png** and the aircraft is called **orbital.png**.

Importing an Image File

From the File menu, choose Import - Import to Library, then select the sky image. To see if the operation succeeded, click on the library icon that can be found in the little toolbar between the timeline and the Properties (second from the bottom).

Right-click on the image and choose Properties. Check the option Export for ActionScript. You can leave the Export to Frame 1 checked (it automatically checks it if you check the first one). Below you will see an input box called Class that shows the name of the file by default. Change it to **SkyBg**. Make sure that the base class just below it shows **flash.display.BitmapData**. Then you can click Ok to close this dialog.

Click on the Layer 1, Frame 1, and open the Actions dialog. Let us start by importing some useful modules:

```
import flash.display.BitmapData;
import flash.display.Sprite;
```

```
import flash.utils.Timer;
```

Next, let us define a variable containing a reference to our image:

```
var tile:BitmapData = new SkyBg(550, 700);
```

Next we'll add an object of type **Sprite** that will allow us to change the way we display the tile more easily. Add the following code:

```
// Create the sprite
var skySprite:Sprite = new Sprite();
// Draw the tile on it
skySprite.graphics.beginBitmapFill(tile);
skySprite.graphics.drawRect(0, 0, tile.width,
                                tile.height);
skySprite.graphics.endFill();
// Add it to the scene so that we can see it
addChild(skySprite);
```

Now test the program. You should see a portion of the sky displayed.

Next, add the following function that will display the sky sprite at a given vertical position on the stage.

```
function displaySprite(ypos)
{
    skySprite.y = ypos;
}
```

We need to define the speed at which we want the sky to be moving, and a variable to keep track of the current position of the sky. You can add these at the top just below the definition of the tile:

```
var speed = 1; var absy = -tile.height;
```

Next, we must add a timer event that will call a function repeatedly to display the sky at a changing position. First, we define a function that handles the movement of the sky in one step,

```
function scrollLayers(event:TimerEvent)
{
    displaySprite(absy);
    absy = absy+speed;
    if (absy>= 0)
    {
        absy = -tile.height;
    }
}
```

Then, we define a timer object with a parameter representing the number of milliseconds for the repetition, and to which we provide this function as a callback.

```
var scroll_timer:Timer = new Timer(5);
scroll_timer.addEventListener(TimerEvent.TIMER,
                              scrollLayers);
scroll_timer.start();
```

Test the application now. It is almost complete in functionality, except for the fact that we need an extra piece of the tile to be added to the screen at the beginning. Add the following line to the definition of the sprite, between the **beginBitmapFill** and **endBitmapFill**, right after the first rectangle:

```
skySprite.graphics.drawRect(0, tile.height,
    tile.width,
    2*tile.height - this.stage.stageHeight);
```

Test the application again - this time it should be doing what we intended it to. Save your work before closing the program.

Displaying the ship

Add a new layer and place it below the background layer in the same scene. Call this layer "ship".

Just like before, import the image of the ship (orbital.png) to the library and create a class for it called OrbitalMv (just like you did for the sky) derived from BitmapData. Click on the ship layer, the first frame, and go to the Actions dialog.

Declare a variable called shipImg of type BitmapData containing a reference to an object of type OrbitalMv created with dimensions 206x397, or whatever numbers represent the original dimensions of the ship image. Next, declare a variable called shipSprite of type Sprite containing a reference to a simple sprite object (just like for the sky). Add a rectangle to this sprite using the variable shipImg and its dimensions. Add the sprite as a child to the stage.

Run the application. You should be able to see the ship, but it is probably too big for our purposes.

Resizing the ship

In the next step, we'll adjust the size of the ship to something that suits the application. For this, let us change the dimensions of the sprite first. So, instead of the width and height of the original image, use 100 and 200 (if your original image was of similar size as described before, the sprite should now display about a quarter of the size ship, half on each side). Run the program again to see the effect.

The displayed image is indeed of the size we want, but it is not resized, only cropped instead. To resize it, we will need to declare a transformation matrix. Add the following code before drawing the rectangle:

```
var sclMatrix = new flash.geom.Matrix();
sclMatrix.identity();
sclMatrix.scale(0.2, 0.2);
```

This will create a matrix that we can use to scale the bitmap data that we use to create the rectangle, but shrinking it to 5 times smaller. Add this new variable as a second parameter to the **beginBitmapFill** function call. Run the program again to see the effect. The ship should now be the right size, but displayed multiple times. This is because the size of the rectangle is larger than the size of the scaled ship. Just adjust the size of the rectangle to 40x80 and the ship should look fine. You may have to adjust the scaling factors 0.2 and 0.2 to whatever fits your image onto a rectangle of size 40x80. You can calculate them by dividing the dimensions of the sprite (40 and 80) by the dimensions of your image. The scaling factor does not need to be the same over **x** as over **y**.

Since we're going to have many objects to move around on the screen, let's add the following useful function:

```
function moveTo(spriteObj, valx, valy)
{
    spriteObj.x = valx;
    spriteObj.y = valy;
}
```

Let's find a good position for the ship on the screen. Given that we'll be moving it around, we should start from the bottom and somewhere in the middle.

Click on the top bar of the Actions window to minimize it. Now

you should be able to see the stage design area again. If we don't want to guess, let's draw a small rectangle in the place where we want to display the ship. Then switch to the selection tool (arrow, top of the drawing toolbar) and select this rectangle. In the properties area to the right you should see some information about where this rectangle is located. Write down the X and Y coordinates. You can use them for the ship. Once this is done, erase the rectangle by selecting it and hitting the delete key.

Go back to the Actions dialog and make sure that you are still in the ship layer. Call the function **moveTo** with the first parameter being the **shipSprite**, then two more with the coordinates that you wrote down. You can adjust these later if it doesn't look quite right. We can also calculate that the stage is 550 pixels wide, the ship is 40 pixels wide, if we calculate the difference and divide by 2, we obtain a value (255) that should be a good **x** coordinate for placing the ship.

Moving the ship

Now we need to add some mobility to the ship. For that we need to add an event listener for keyboard type of events, and a function to handle it. Since the event is not necessarily happening on the ship sprite itself, but is generally related to the stage, that is the object that needs to be listening to this event. Add the following code to the ship frame:

```
stage.addEventListener(KeyboardEvent.KEY_DOWN,
                       keyDownHandler);
```

```
function keyDownHandler(event:
                        KeyboardEvent):void
{
    trace("keyboard down event");
    trace("key code: " + event.keyCode);
}
```

Next to the Timeline you will see a tab called OUTPUT. Click on it, and then run the program. Make sure to click in the application window first to make sure that it is in focus. Try the arrow keys to see what the code is for each of them. Let's create some constants for these codes, so we don't have to remember them every time. Add the following code before defining the event listener:

```
const arrow_up:Number = 38;
const arrow_down:Number = 40;
const arrow_left:Number = 37;
const arrow_right:Number = 39;
```

Next, add the following function right after the function **moveTo**. This will be moving an object horizontally by a given number of pixels:

```
function moveHor(spriteObj, t)
{
    spriteObj.x +=  t;
}
```

Add a similar function called **moveVert** that moves the object vertically by that number of pixels.

Now we can add a **switch** statement (it works like in C++) to handle these arrow keys. Comment out the **trace** function calls in the keyboard handler function and add the following:

```
switch (event.keyCode)
{
    case arrow_up:
        moveVert(shipSprite, -3);
        break;
```

Complete this function with the 3 remaining cases and close all the braces. Test the program. Your ship should be moving around when the arrow keys are pressed. Note: if you want the movement to be faster and smoother, you would need to add a timer kind of event listener (like for the sky) that moves the ship in one given direction. Then the key down even would trigger it to start, and the key up even would trigger it to stop.

Now we'd like to prevent the ship from getting out of the screen. Let's restrict the movement to 10 pixels from the border all around. For this, let's add a condition to the movement down that says:

```
if (shipSprite.y <= stage.stageHeight -
    shipSprite.height -13)
{
```

just before the movement of the sprite. Close the brace before the break statement. Add similar conditions for all the other cases.

Timer movement

Before we add other objects, let's change the movement of the ship sprite to use a timer event. For this, first make a copy of the function **keyDownHandler** and call it **KeyDownHandlerSimple**. We'll keep it as reference.

Add a timer object with the following code:

```
var shipTimer:Timer = new Timer(3);
shipTimer.addEventListener(TimerEvent.TIMER,
                           moveShip);
shipTimer.start();
var shipDir = 0;
```

Note that we are also declaring a global variable that will let us know which direction the ship is supposed to be moving in. Change the name of the function **keyDownHandler** to **moveShip** (the callback for our event above). Change the movement to 1 pixel at a time and change all the conditions appropriately (13 becomes 11, for example). Change the expression in the switch statement from (**event.keyCode**) to (**shipDir**). Change the parameter to **event:TimerEvent** : this is the type of parameter needed for the timer events.

Let us now define a new function to be used as callback for the arrow keys being pressed. Define a new function called **keyDownHandler** with the same **event** parameter as the first one (copy it from the simple version). The first thing to do is to assign to the variable **shipDir** the value of the **event.keyCode** which was used in the **switch** before. In this version, we need to start the timer, but only if it isn't already on. For this, add the following conditional:

```
if (!shipTimer.running)
{
    shipTimer.start();
}
```

This conditional tests first if the timer is not yet active, and activates it in that case. Now we need another callback function that stops the timer when the key is released. For this, add the following line right next to the one adding the **KEY_DOWN** event:

```
stage.addEventListener(KeyboardEvent.KEY_UP,
                       keyUpHandler);
```

Then after the function keyDownHandler add the following:

```
function keyUpHandler(event:KeyboardEvent)
{
    shipTimer.stop();
}
```

This function will simply stop the timer when called.

Other objects

Create two images for two types of objects that will appear in the game. One of them will be an enemy to avoid, and the other one will be a friendly object that the player should try to collect. Figure 17 shows an example of the two images. The parachute is the friendly object, while the helicopter is the enemy. We'll assume here that the two images you created are called **parachute.png** and **helicopter.png**.

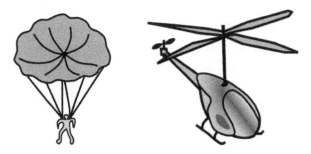

Figure 17. Examples of two types of objects to be used in the game

The first one we'll use to represent people jumping with

parachutes that we need to save, and the others helicopters that we need to avoid. Import them both to the library and give them the class names `ParachuteMv` and `HelicopterMv`.

Add a class called `MySprite` and save it in a file called `MySprite.as`. Start the file by adding the package information and importing necessary modules:

```
package
{
    import flash.display.BitmapData;
    import flash.display.Sprite;
    import flash.display.Stage;
    import flash.utils.Timer;
    import flash.geom.Matrix;
}
```

Let's start writing a class whose instances will represent objects in the game with somewhat similar behavior. The class will contain a sprite member that will store and display the critter's avatar, and an option to designate which game object it represents. The object is meant to be animated; thus, we'll need a speed for it and a timer. Since this is a vertical scroller game and these objects have only vertical mobility, we only need one value for the speed. We'll need to store the size of the original image, and the size of the sprite box for collision detection purposes.

Add the following declaration to the file, inside the package.

```
public class MySprite
{
    // Define some constants for the type
    const PARACHUTE_TY = 0,
          HELICOPTER_TY = 1,
          WIDTH = 50;
    // Class properties or attributes
    public var theSprite;
```

```
    // parachute or helicopter
    public var type:int;

    var mySpeed:int;        // speed of movement

    // The bounding box
    public var boxw:int, boxh:int;

    // Size of the original image
    var bmpw:int, bmph:int;

    var myTimer:Timer;
    var parent:Stage; // We'll store it in here
}
```

A class needs a constructor. For this class, we'll need a pointer to the stage so that we can store a reference in the class, and a parameter for the type of game object that we create. The second parameter can have a default value, the first one cannot. Let's start by assigning values to the easiest attributes.

```
public function MySprite(theStage:Stage,
                    givenType = PARACHUTE_TY)
{
    parent = theStage;
    theSprite = new Sprite();
    type = givenType;
    mySpeed = 0;
}
```

In the constructor we need to create a bitmap object based on the type of object (parachute or helicopter), and then build a sprite from it. We'll assume here that the images are not of the size that will be displayed on the screen and some scaling is required. We'll also assume that the objects have a given width, and that the height will be determined for each type of object based on the proportions of the original image.

Let's start by setting up the bitmap. Add the following code to the constructor and replace the dimensions of the image for each case with the dimensions of your image.

```
var bitmapImg:BitmapData;
boxw = WIDTH; // displayed width of the object
if (type =  = PARACHUTE_TY)
{
    bmpw = 400; // dimensions of the image
    bmph = 400;
    bitmapImg = new ParachuteMv(bmpw,bmph);
    scale = 0.22;
    boxh = 63;
}
else
{
    bmpw = 254; // dimensions of the image
    bmph = 216;
    bitmapImg = new HelicopterMv(bmpw,bmph);
    scale = 0.197;
    boxh = 43;
}
```

Now we need to determine the scaling factor and the vertical dimension of the displayed object. For this, we'll use the rate between the width of the displayed sprite and the width of the original image. Since we've declared both of them as integers, we need to convert one of them to a float so that the operation is done using real numbers. Then by multiplying the scale by the height or the original image, we can obtain the height of the displayed sprite. Add the following code to the constructor:

```
var scale = float(boxw)/bmpw;
boxh = scale * bmph;
```

Then we can use this scale to build a scale matrix to be used to build the sprite from the image:

```
var sclMatrix = new Matrix();
sclMatrix.identity();
sclMatrix.scale(scale, scale);
```

Now this matrix can be used to create the sprite. Once we have the sprite, we need to add it to the stage so that it can be displayed. We'll make it invisible to begin with, so that we can decide later in the game when we want it to become visible.

```
theSprite.graphics.beginBitmapFill(bitmapImg,
                                   sclMatrix);
theSprite.graphics.drawRect(0, 0, boxw, boxh);
theSprite.graphics.endFill();
parent.addChild(theSprite);
theSprite.visible = false; // We don't want to
                           // show it right away.
```

The constructor should now be complete for what we plan to do with this object. Next, we'll add a function to activate one of these objects in the game. These objects are meant to be used dynamically: they appear at the top of the stage, as the ship presumably arrives in their vicinity, and disappear at the bottom of the stage or are captured by the player. The disappearing objects don't have to be deleted. Instead, we can reuse them to make new objects appear at the top. Thus, we need functions to activate and deactivate the object.

In the activating function, we will place the object at a random position within the stage width and make it start form the top. We must also make the sprite visible.

In the function **deactivate**, all we have to do is make the sprite invisible. It's also prudent to reset its coordinates and speed.

```
// Call it to activate the object
public function activate()
{
```

```
    // Start it from a random position
    theSprite.x = (parent.stageWidth - boxw) *
                  Math.random();
    // and with a random speed
    mySpeed = 1+3*Math.random();
    // start from outside the screen
    theSprite.y = - boxh;
    theSprite.visible = true;
}

// Call to hide the object
public function deactivate()
{
    theSprite.visible = false;
    theSprite.x = 0;
    theSprite.y = 0;
    mySpeed = 0;
}
```

The next function we need is one that we can call in each frame to move the sprite to a new position. As a precaution, we will only move the sprite if it is visible. If the sprite gets off the stage after the move, then we make it invisible.

```
// Call it to move the sprite
public function move()
{
    if (theSprite.visible)
    {
        theSprite.y += mySpeed;
    }
    if (theSprite.y>parent.stageHeight)
    {
        // getting out of the screen
        theSprite.visible = false;
    }
}
```

Next, we will write some functions for collision detection with another sprite. We first start by a function checking if we have collision over the x coordinate. Then another one checking for collision over the y coordinate. In this case, we will consider that the second sprite is a point, so we only take into account its position and not its dimensions. Both of these will check for the position of the second sprite being inside the interval occupied by the sprite belonging to the object in each coordinate.

```
// Collision on the x coordinate only.
// Not a public function.
function collidesX(what:Sprite):Boolean
{
    if (theSprite.x <= what.x)
    {
        return (what.x - theSprite.x <= boxw);
    }
    else
    {
        return (theSprite.x - what.x <=
            what.width);
    }
}

// Collision on the y coordinate only.
// Not a public function.
function collidesY(what:Sprite):Boolean
{
    if (theSprite.y <= what.y)
    {
        return (what.y - theSprite.y <= boxh);
    }
    else
    {
        return (theSprite.y - what.y <=
            what.height);
    }
}
```

These two functions are not public because they are not meant to be called by themselves from outside the class. The next function checks for collision in both coordinates by calling the previous two functions, and this will be the public function.

```
public function collides(what:Sprite):Boolean
{
    return (collidesX(what) &&
            collidesY(what));
}
```

To use this class in our program we need to import it. Create a new layer in the stage called **parachutes** and copy the following code into the Actions area:

```
import MySprite;
var parch:mySprite = new mySprite(stage, 0);
var helic:mySprite = new mySprite(stage, 1);
```

This creates two objects in the stage, a parachute and a helicopter. We need a function that will move both of them in the next frame of the game. Let's call it **moveFoe**. This function will also check if any of the sprites has become invisible in the last update and activate it again. It will move the two objects, then check for collision with the player's ship. If any of them collides with it, then it is deactivated. The code is shown on the next page.

This function will not be called directly in the application, but linked to a timer such that it can be called regularly. For this we need to create a timer, and then add this function as a callback for the timer event. Add the following code either before or after the function:

```
var gameTimer:Timer = new Timer(45);
gameTimer.addEventListener(TimerEvent.TIMER,
                            moveFoe);
gameTimer.start();

function moveFoe(event:TimerEvent)
{
```

```
    if (!parch.theSprite.visible)
    {
        parch.activate();
    }
    if (!helic.theSprite.visible)
    {
        helic.activate();
    }
    parch.move();
    helic.move();
    if (parch.collides(shipSprite))
    {
        parch.deactivate();
    }
    if (helic.collides(shipSprite))
    {
        helic.deactivate();
    }
}
```

Test the application now to see that it works.

On Your Own

Create an array of size 10 and fill it with objects of type
MySprite, half of them parachutes and half of them
helicopters. Modify the function **moveFoe** such that it
reactivates all the objects in the array that are not visible,
moves all of them, and then checks for collision. Each of these
actions is done twice in the current version of the function: for
the **parch** object and for the **helic** object. Each of these
double calls will be replaced by a **for** loop going over all the
elements of the array and calling the function for each of them.
Alternatively, a single loop can contain 3 function calls for each
object.

A second change consists of implementing a score and
modifying it each time there is a collision with one of the

objects. The player could also be given a number of lives, and the game could remove one every time there is a collision with the wrong type of objects (helicopters, in this case). Once the number of lives gets to 0, then the next collision with a helicopter causes the game to be lost. In that case, the **gameTimer** must be stopped, and a message displayed for the player.

5.4 A Path-Based Animated Game

We will now proceed to another tutorial creating a game based on an animated loop where a set of objects move along a given path, and that involves collision detection.

In this tutorial we will implement a ball shooting game similar to such games as Zuma or Blackbeard's Island. The idea is that the player controls one or more cannons shooting balls of various colors. The stage at every level features an outlined path and a stream of randomly generated balls is coming along it at a constant speed. The path ends on a particular place of the stage marked by a special icon, as for example, a burning fire. If the stream of incoming balls reaches the end of the path, the game is lost. The player can shoot balls from the cannon towards the incoming stream. When such an action creates a continuous chain of 3 or more balls of the same color, they are eliminated from the stream. The goal is to eliminate all the balls coming in and not let the stream reach the end of the path. We will call this game Stream Shoot.

Here is a list of objects we will need in the game:

- A cannon object controlled by the user through mouse movement. The cannon should be able to shoot, action that will be related to a mouse click event.
- A ball to be shot by the cannon. The initial position and velocity of the ball will depend on the orientation of the cannon. Once the ball hits the target or is lost, it is reactivated inside the cannon object. The ball's movement will be handled by a dedicated timer.
- A stream of balls coming into the stage along a given path. Their behavior is fairly complex as parts of the stream might be moving and others not at any given time. Their

movement also needs a dedicated timer. The stream will be organized as an array of ball objects.

Tutorial 5

In this tutorial we'll implement one level of the game Stream Shoot. We'll assume that we are working with balls of four colors: red, green, blue, yellow.

Preparation

Just as before, the first thing to prepare is the set of resources. We will need to create images for the balls in each color. If you intend to implement a more comprehensive version of this game, you may want to prepare images for balls that are marked by special flags that give them bonus properties in the game. The classic flags would be

- an arrow back, that causes the stream to be rolled backward by a given amount when that ball is eliminated,
- a bomb, causing the ball to explode when hit and eliminate all the balls in a given radius around it,
- a pause flag (two vertical bars) causing the stream to either halt movement altogether or slow it down when the ball is eliminated.

We'll implement these three features in this tutorial. Start by creating an image for the ball in each color, of size 100x100, called `blueball.png`, and so on. Then from each of these images, create three more containing the flags described above, called `blueback.png`, `bluebomb.png`, and `bluestop.png`, respectively, and similarly for the other colors. Figure 18 below shows the example used in this book for the four original images, as well as the three flagged ones.

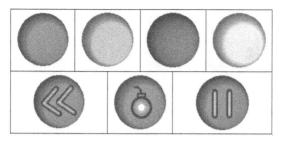

Figure 18. Images used in the Stream Shoot game

Then we also need an image for the cannon that will be shooting the balls, keeping in mind that it will need to be able to display the ball it is about to shoot. We also have to take into account the fact that the cannon will be rotating towards the direction of the ball that is being shot, which means that the ball must be attached to it in some way and the rotation should be consistent with its relative position with respect to the cannon. The easiest way to deal with it is to place the ball in the center of the cannon, that way the ball doesn't need to rotate at all. Here we'll use an image where the ball is not in the center, to discuss how we can deal with that situation. In this tutorial we will use two bitmaps for the cannon: a wheel that stays in place, and a shaft that rotates with the direction of the shot. Traditionally some other place on the screen shows the next ball that will be available to shoot, so the player can plan for it. Figure 19 shows the objects that we'll use for this purpose:

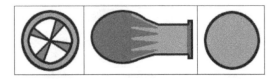

Figure 19. Images for the cannon wheel, shaft, and next ball holder

Then we need an image for the path that the stream of balls will be taking coming into the stage. This can be done directly in Flash using vector drawing, if the programmer trusts their skill enough, or it can be drawn with a different program and then imported directly to the stage. As this object is not going to be interactive, either way would serve the purpose.

Finally, you may want to create a clipart image for the background, or something more sophisticated, depending on your artistic skill and ambition. Figure 20 shows a clipart used in this tutorial for the background and a second one for the path. The end of the path marks a hole where balls will be falling once they reach the end.

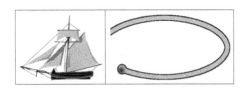

Figure 20. Background and path

Once the images are prepared, create an ActionScript 3 project and set up the stage to the size and color that you want. Import the background image, the path, and any other decorations directly to the stage, and not to the library. Position these elements and resize them the way you want them to look in the game.

Import all the other images to the library. Note that the import action allows for multiple resources to be added at one time. Make each of them available for ActionScript and give them class names that are easy to remember or to connect to the name of the image. For this part, the classes need to be created individually.

Path Coordinates

The next items to acquire are the coordinates of the centerline of the path. We need a relatively high density of coordinates following the center of the path to make the movement of the balls look smooth. It is recommended to have them spaced out at an interval at most equal to the radius of the ball.

There are two ways to generate these coordinates. First, by taking direct measurements in the image. For this, you need a program that can give you the x and y coordinates on an image at the current position of the mouse pointer. Flash itself may not be ideal for this, but an image processing application such as Adobe Photoshop or the Gimp can provide this functionality.

The second way is to generate these points using the equation of the curve. For an ellipsis, which is what is shown in Figure 20, let us suppose that c_x and c_y are the coordinated of the center, and that a and b are the small and large radii respectively. Then the equations are

$x = c_x + a \cos(s)$

$y = c_y + b \sin(s)$

where s is a parameter that starts form 0 and goes incrementally up to 2*π, which represents 360 degrees. The center coordinates and radii can be measured directly on the image. The coordinates can be generated in a spreadsheet program like MS Excel or with a small program in any language.

To generate these directly in Flash, we can first add one ball to the stage, dragged to the stage from the Library, in any color. Then we can place it on the path and adjust its dimensions to fit in the stream. After it is converted to a Symbol, it can be given an instance name so that its position on the stage can be controlled in the code. We will be calling it `ballTest`.

After that, moving the ball to the center of the ellipsis, we can write down approximately the values of **cx** and **cy**, and then moving it to the top center and the right center of the path respectively, we can approximate the values of **a** and **b** based on the difference between the **x** and **y** coordinates of the ball and of the center. These values can be adjusted after the code is run based on observations.

Opening the Actions page, the following code will create a sequence of points to control the movement of the stream and store them in the array `coords`. Then it will also walk the object `ballTest` along this path to see if the coordinates have been calculated correctly. For this, we will generate a high density of points on the path and assign each of these points as the coordinates of the `ballTest` object. An issue that arises here is that the process will be too fast and we won't have time to see the ball scanning the path. To slow it down, we need to add a timer that moves it to the next position on the path. Here is the code for this test on a stage of dimensions 700x500:

```
import Math;
import flash.utils.Timer;
var a = 364, b = 211, cx = 296, cy = 240,
    s = 0, alphaStep = Math.PI/100, px, py;
```

```
var myTimer = new Timer(200);
myTimer.addEventListener(TimerEvent.TIMER,
                         makePoint);

function makePoint(event:TimerEvent)
{
    px = cx + a * Math.cos(s);
    py = cy + b * Math.sin(s);
    s = s + alphaStep;
    if (px >= 0 && py >= 0)
    {
        ballTest.x = px;
        ballTest.y = py;
    }
    trace(px, py);
}

myTimer.start();
```

By observing the movement of the ball along the path, one can determine if the coordinates are correct and make adjustments as necessary. When the coordinates have been appropriately set, they can be stored in an array for later use. For that, first determine the quadrant from which the path starts (such as top left) and initialize the variable **s** above with the value corresponding to that. The value 0 corresponds to the center right or the bottom right quadrant. The bottom left quadrant starts with the value π/2. The top right quadrant, which is the one for the path in Figure 20, starts from the value π. The top right quadrant starts with the value 3π/2. Then declare a variable of type **Array** and a variable i equal to 0 to hold the place where the coordinate is going to be stored. Place the code generating the coordinates inside a loop. For every coordinate that was generated with **x** and **y** that are not negative, instead of assigning them as coordinates to **ballTest**, store them in the array at positions i and i+1, and increment the variable i by 2 afterwards. Here is an example of the code, where **coords** is the name of the array variable. The function **push** adds one or more elements to the end of an array.

```
coords.push(px, py);
```

If you have a **Point** class from a previous project, this would be a good place to use it.

Ball Class

Now that we have all the images in place and the coordinates of the path, we can start building the class that will handle the balls. The model we'll use here is a small class handling each individual ball and a container class to handle all the balls that are coming on the path. For the individual ball path, you can start from the class **Tile** from the **Mines** class. These classes have some elements in common as they both need a set of different images to be used for the same object in different situations.

Otherwise declare a class called **Ball** in a separate file and add the attributes **simpleClip**, **backClip**, **stopClip**, and **bombClip** to it. These will represent the sprites for the different images that will be used for the ball. Add a couple of attributes called **centerx** and **centery** for the position of the ball, one for the **size**, and one for the stage called **parent**. Add a couple of public attributes for the **state** and for the **color**. Then in the constructor, add a parameter for the stage, and a parameter for each of these attributes and assign to each attribute the value of the corresponding parameter.

We are going to need a function that creates a sprite from a bitmap image that is also capable of adapting to a size that is different from the original image. The function **makeSprite** defined earlier in the game of **Yahtzee** will be suitable for this purpose. Copy that function into the class **Ball**.

To create all of the sprites that make a ball of a particular color work, we need to call the function **makeSprite** with a bitmap created from the class defined for each image and store the result in the class attribute. The code is almost the same for all of the colors, except for the name of the classes used to create the bitmap variables initially. To optimize the amount of code we need to write, we're going to write one function that receives the four bitmaps as an array in a parameter. This is what the function looks like; the function **positionClip** is copied from the class **Tile** from the **Mines** project:

```
function makeClips(bmpArray)
{
    simpleClip = makeSprite(bmpArray[0], 100,
                                    size);
    parent.addChild(simpleClip);
    positionClip(simpleClip);
}
```

Replace 100 with the size of your original image, and add similar lines for each of the sprites to be created. Now we can write a function specifically for the color red:

```
function makeRedBall()
{
    var bmpArray = new Array(4);
    bmpArray[0] = new RedBallBmp();
    bmpArray[1] = new RedBackBmp();
    bmpArray[2] = new RedBombBmp();
    bmpArray[3] = new RedStopBmp();
    makeClips(bmpArray);
}
```

Write a similar function for each of the other colors. At last, we can piece together these functions into one that can be called from the constructor based on the color received as parameter:

```
function makeClipsByColor()
{
    switch (color)
    {
        case 0:
            makeRedBall();
            break;
    }
}
```

Here we'll assume that 0 means red, and 1, 2, and 3 mean blue, green, and yellow respectively. We will let the reader complete all the other cases. Call this function from the constructor.

The last thing that we need for now in the class **Ball** is to adapt the function **setState** that was written in the class **Tile** in the project **Mines** to the attributes that are defined in this class. The idea in this function is the same: depending on the value of **state**, set the right clip as **visible** and all the others as invisible. Call this function from the constructor. Note that if we call this function with a value other than the four states for which we have a defined sprite or clip, then the effect is to make the ball invisible.

At this point, the class can be tested by declaring one object of this class in the Actions dialog of the project. Place it somewhere in the middle of the stage, then try different colors and states in the constructor to see if they have the desired effect.

The Stream Class

Let's create a container class for the balls that moves them along the path. For this, add a class to the project called **Stream**. Import the class **Ball** we've defined in it, the **Timer** from **flash.utils** and **TimerEvent** from **flash.events**.

Declare the class attributes **ballArray**, **ballCount**, **coords**, **moveTimer** and **parent**. In the constructor, add one parameter for the stage and assign it to the **parent** attribute. Then assign to **ballCount** a value that would be a good initial count of balls to be active in that particular level. We'll start here with 100, and the number can be adjusted later or redefined depending on the level. Initialize the **ballArray** as an **Array** object with **ballCount** as parameter. Initialize the timer with code similar to what was used in the stage. Add a class attribute called **ballSize** and initialize it with the value used in the stage for the size. Then this attribute can be used everywhere in this class instead of the constant. Finally, add a **for** loop where you create a new object of type **Ball** for every element of the array, with the size that was used in the stage for testing purposes. Assign it some negative coordinates that are less than the negative of the size of the ball, to prevent them from being visible on the screen.

Let's move the array of points from the stage area into the class **Stream**. Add a function called **makePoints** and copy the code creating the points from the main stage area into this function. Copy all the relevant variables from the stage into the class function. The center coordinates and the two radii **a** and **b** might be useful as class attributes, so declare them as such and initialize them in the constructor. All of the others can be declared as local variables in the function. Import the **Math** module too. We'll make a small change here, to make the movement of the stream look more continuous: instead of testing if the coordinates generated in the loop are positive, test that they are greater than or equal to minus the ball size. This way we'll see the balls enter the stage progressively instead of appearing on it all of a sudden. We also need to store a counter for the number of points that we have. Declare a class attribute called **pointNum**, initialize it as 0, and increment it by 1 for every pair a coordinates added to the **coords** array in the function **makePoints**. Then call this function from the constructor.

Now let us make the stream of balls work. To plan ahead, we'll activate the balls starting from the end of the array going backwards. When a ball is eliminated form the screen, we'll delete the object and shift the remaining balls backward afterward. We'll need an attribute for the lowest index in the stream of any active ball. Every time enough space is freed on the stream for a new ball to come into the stage, we'll activate it by decrementing this index. Let's call it **firstMoving**. Declare this as a class attribute and initialize its value with **ballCount**.

We will also need a public attribute in the class **Ball** for the index of the geometrical point in the stream where the ball is situated. Call this attribute **spot**. First, we need a function in the class **Ball** that will place the object at a new position and set the **spot** parameter accordingly. Note that this function needs to move all the clips or the ball to the new position. Here is this function:

```
public function move(px, py, sp)
{
    centerx = px;
    centery = py;
    spot = sp;
    positionClip(simpleClip);
    positionClip(backClip);
    positionClip(bombClip);
    positionClip(stopClip);
}
```

Then in the class **Stream**, we'll add a function moving one ball to a new **spot**. This function will increment the **spot** first, then get the coordinates of a new point from 2 times the **spot** number, and the index following it, because we have two coordinates for every point. The function is shown next.

```
function moveBall(bl)
{
    var sp = bl.spot;
    if (sp+1 < pointNum)
    {
        sp++;
        bl.move(coords[2*sp], coords[2*sp+1],
                sp+1);
        return true;
    }
    else
    {
        return false;
    }
}
```

Note that this function returns **true** if the ball is moved to a valid position on the path, and **false** if it isn't, because the ball has reached the end of the path. This can be used in the function moving the whole stream to decide when the game is lost.

Then we need a function that checks if a condition is fulfilled to activate another ball and start moving it on the path. Let's see what this condition might be. If no ball is active on the stage at that point (the game has just started), which can be determined by the fact that **firstMoving** is still equal to **ballCount**, then a ball should be activated no matter what. Otherwise, we must calculate the distance between the position of the active ball of lowest index on the stage and the coordinate of the entry point in the **coords** array. If this distance is at least as big as the size of the ball, then we have enough space to activate a new ball. Figure 21 illustrates this situation.

Activating a ball means moving it to the right position on the stage and decrementing the variable **firstMoving**, providing that its value is not yet 0. This function is shown on the next page. We also provide two additional helping functions for computing the simple distance, and the distance between two points in the **coords** array given by the point index, which we may use again later.

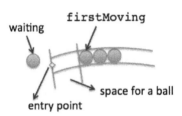

Figure 21 Situation where the next ball can be activated

```
function distance(x1, y1, x2, y2)
{
    return Math.sqrt((x1-x2)*(x1-x2) +
                     (y1-y2)*(y1-y2));
}
```

```
function distancePt(p1, p2)
{
    return distance(coords[2*p1],
                    coords[2*p1+1],
                    coords[2*p2],
                    coords[2*p2+1]);
}

function checkActivate()
{
    var d = ballSize;
    if (firstMoving < ballCount)
    {
        var sp = ballArray[firstMoving].spot;
        d = distance(sp, 0);
    }
    if (d >= ballSize && firstMoving > 0)
    {
        firstMoving--;
        ballArray[firstMoving].move(coords[0],
            coords[1], 0);
    }
}
```

We can now piece together these two functions in a function called **moveStream**. We start by moving forward all the balls from **firstMoving** to **ballCount-1** by one path point. If any of the balls reaches the end of the path (and of the array of coordinates), in which case the **moveBall** function returns **false**, then we deactivate all the balls from that position to the end of the stream and update **ballCount** accordingly. After that, we check if we have created enough space to add a new ball by calling the function **checkActivate**. The function is on the next page.

Finally, we can add a parameter called event to this function and add it to the timer as the callback function for the timer event. Attaching the event to the timer can be done in the constructor. At the end of the constructor function, after everything has been initialized properly, call the function **start** on the timer.

```
function moveStream()
{
    for (var i = firstMoving; i<ballCount; i++)
    {
        if (! moveBall(ballArray[i]))
        {
            for (var j = i; j<ballCount; j++)
            {
                ballArray[j].setState(4);
                ballArray[j] = null;
            }
            ballCount = i;
        }
    }
    checkActivate();
}
```

We now have enough elements in the project to test the functionality we've added so far. Going back to the stage, in the Actions window, comment out all the existing code except for the importing statements and then import the **Stream** class. Declare an object of this class. Short of syntax errors, this declaration should be sufficient to create all the objects needed to display the stream and activate it. Cross your fingers and proceed to the test.

The application should be running pretty nicely, but one problem might become apparent from observing what happens. It is quite probable that the points on the ellipsis are not spaced out evenly. This is because we have generated them using a constant angle. If the points happen to be along the elongated side of the ellipsis, then they will be further apart than if they were along the shorter side. Thus, depending on the quadrant you start from, the balls will either overlap over some portions of the path, or not stick together on others. Figure 22 shows an example of this issue.

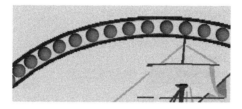

Figure 22. Uneven spacing of the balls on the path

To avoid this, one can initially generate the coordinates with a much higher density, then write them in the coordinates array at an almost constant distance. The idea is to generate a large number of points and only store some of them in the cords array. For each newly generated point, we will check the distance between it and the previously recorded one. When this distance becomes equal to the ball radius, or some other constant increment, we will record the new point.

For this, make the angle increment **alphaStep** much smaller. Then have a constant that you want to be used for the increment, **delta**, declared as local to this function (this would be equal to the ball radius or a fraction of it), and a variable **increment** initialized as **−1**. Modify the conditional inside the loop in the function **makePoints** the following way:

```
if (px >= -ballSize && py >= -ballSize)
{
    if (increment == -1)
    {
        increment = delta;
    }
```

```
else
{
    increment +=
        distance(px,py,oldpx,oldpy);
}
if (increment >= delta)
{
    coords.push(px, py);
    pointNum++;
    increment -= delta;
}
oldpx = px;
oldpy = py;
}
```

Here we're progressively computing the distance along the path by adding the distance between consecutively generated points with a small constant angle. Figure 23 illustrates this concept. When this distance becomes greater than or equal to the interval **delta**, we store the current point in the coordinates array. Instead of restarting the increment back from 0, we subtract the value **delta** from it. This helps avoiding round-off errors. On the path shown in Figure 20, with the value of **delta** equal to **ballSize** divided by 10.0 and a total of 5000 generated points (not all of them stored), the tested movement of the balls was smooth with no apparent gaps. The total number of stored points out of the 5000 is only 581. A factor in this is the fact that part of the ellipse is cut off from the screen.

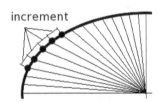

Figure 23. Computing the distance along the curve incrementally

Before moving on to the next subject, the point generating process needs to stop when reaching the end point on the path. This happens before an entire ellipsis is generated. In order to do that, one must first find the approximate coordinates of that point. For that, you can drag any ball object from the library to the stage, resize it and move it to the end of the path, and then write down its coordinates in the properties area. In the path used here, these coordinates are approximately 50x400. Then you can add a condition similar to the following code inside the **for** loop generating the points:

```
if (coords.length > 100 && px <50)
{
    break;
}
```

First we are testing if enough points have already been generated on the path, because the area of the ellipsis at the beginning of the path will be in a similar vicinity over **x**. Then we test one of the coordinates for reaching the point determined above by measurement. If that is the case, we break out of the **for** loop.

Randomizing the Colors

The next step that we can take in the project is to randomize the colors of the balls. For this, we can simply generate a random value for the color in the desired range. For example, let's label by **colorNum** the number of colors we can use on that level (four in our case). Given that the function **random** generates a value between 0 and 1, then the color can be generated with

```
color = int(Math.random()*colorNum);
```

This instruction belongs to the constructor of the class **Stream**, after which the **color** parameter in the function call creating the **Ball** objects can use this value. This is working fine, but the effect is to create a stream of colors that are mixed up more than we expect in such a game, especially in beginning levels. More importantly, we cannot control the degree of randomness in the colors to create the effect of increasingly difficult levels in the game.

For a better model, let's set the variable **color** randomly to begin with, and then have another variable to control when it is changed randomly again. Declare a class attribute called **randomness** and give it an experimental value between 0 and 1, such as 0.4. Then we'll generate a random value (no need to store it) and if it is greater than this variable, we'll change the value of the **color** with a new random call. Thus, the value assigned to the variable **randomness** represents the probability that the color will stay the same from one ball in the stream to the next.

```
if (Math.random() > randomness)
    color = int(Math.random()*colorNum);
```

Removing a Ball

This is the essential operation that will allow us to shoot balls at the stream and eliminate them. What we need to accomplish here is an operation that is focused on one ball in the stream, supposedly hit by a shot ball, where we check to see if there are at least two balls the same color as it (a third one will presumably be the ball that was shot towards the stream), and eliminate them from the stream. Then if the balls on the two sides of those that were eliminated have matching colors, they are pulled together. If they form a sequence of at least 3 balls of the same color, then they are also eliminated and the procedure is repeated while these conditions are met. If the balls on the two sides do not match, then there are two things that can happen based on the implementation: either the balls are pulled together anyway, but none are eliminated, or the balls remain in place until the stream catches up with them. We will discuss the second implementation here, as it seems to be more popular.

To implement a feature where the continuous part of the stream is moving, but other balls stranded further down the path are not, we need to add a class attribute called **lastMoving**. This will represent the largest index in the stream array of any ball that is moving, and is the counterpart of the variable **firstMoving**. We can initialize it with the value **ballCount-1** in the constructor. Then we need to change the function **moveStream** replacing the continuation condition for the first **for** loop with "i <= lastMoving". In the same function, after the balls have been moved, we need to check whether the position of the last moving ball is close enough to the next one in the stream. If that's the case, then the moving stream need to connect with the next contiguous sequence of balls that weren't moving, and start their motion (pushing them along). For this, we need to update the value of **lastMoving** to include all the balls that were continuously connected to the first static one on the path.

Before we proceed any further, let's update the function **checkActivate** with these new elements in mind. The first conditional in this function checks if there is a stream of balls already moving on the path and computes the distance between the first active ball and the first point on the path if that is the case. In a situation where matching balls have been removed, leaving the ones closest to the beginning of the path static, we don't need to compute this distance and we can activate the next ball that would be entering the path without checking. This situation can be described by the fact that the value of **lastMoving** has now become less than **firstMoving**, because **firstMoving** will have been updated to reflect the balls that were deleted. So, we'll modify this test to include this situation. Replace "**firstMoving < ballCount**" with "**firstMoving <= lastMoving**". Note that since **lastMoving** is in all situations less than **ballCount**, this test also covers the previous situation.

The second change needs to be implemented inside the second conditional. Here, if we need to activate the next ball, we decrement **firstMoving** and then call the function **move** on this ball. In the situation where the first ball on the path is not immediately next to the beginning of the path, we might have a set of null elements (deleted balls) in the **ballArray** between the first non-active ball and the first active one. Thus, **firstMoving** needs to skip all of those positions until it finds the first non-active ball. Replace the instruction decrementing **firstMoving** with the following loop:

```
do {
    firstMoving--;
} while (firstMoving > 0 &&
        !ballArray[firstMoving]);
```

To avoid having to check the distance for all the consecutive balls, we can use a scheme where we leave the places of the eliminated balls empty in the array unless the colors on the ends of the two sub-streams match and they can be pulled together. Thus, when the moving part of the stream connects with a static sequence, we can decide which balls to start moving again simply by checking the null pointers. At that point, though, it makes more sense to shift the entire contiguous sequence that had been static backward in the stream array, such that the balls that are moving form a contiguous sequence. This way we avoid having to shift the balls in the array until it becomes necessary.

To accomplish this, let's first add a function that shifts a contiguous sequence of balls in the array (and not on the path) backwards from one index to another. Since this is an operation that will be needed in more than one place, it makes sense to have a separate function for it. As a failsafe, if the index where we're trying to move the sequence is not before the one we're moving it from, then the operation will not work, so we start by testing for this condition. A shift forward operation is also possible, but it isn't something that we need in this program. Here is this function:

```
public function shiftSequence(to, from)
{
    var i;
    if (to < from)
    {
        for (i = from; i<ballCount &&
                    ballArray[i]; i++) {
            ballArray[to + i - from] =
                ballArray[i];
            ballArray[i] = null;
        }
        if (lastMoving >= to)
        {
            lastMoving = to + i - from - 1;
        }
    }
}
```

```
    else
    {
        for (i = to; i<ballCount &&
                     ballArray[i]; i++);
        lastMoving = i-1;
    }
}
```

The **else** part of the condition is dealing with the situation where the sequence to be moved is already in the place where it needs to move. Given the fact that we're calling this function when the moving part of the stream catches up with a static part of it, in that case we still need to update the value of the variable **lastMoving** to allow this new sequence to be integrated with the previous one.

Let's add the second function and then call it from the function **moveStream** right after the call to **checkActivate**. In this function, we are basically checking if the part of the stream that is moving is catching up with a static sequence in the stream. We can consider them close enough if the distance between the position of the last moving ball and the first non-null one that is not moving is less than or equal to the size of the ball objects. If that is the case, then we can call the function we have defined above.

```
function checkMergeStreams()
{
    var i = lastMoving+1, p1, p2, j;
    while (i<ballCount && !ballArray[i])
    {
        i++;
    }
    if (i<ballCount)
    {
        p1 = ballArray[lastMoving].spot;
        p2 = ballArray[i].spot;
```

```
    if (distance(p1, p2) <= ballSize)
    {
        shiftSequence(lastMoving+1, i);
    }
  }
}
```

Let's add a public function called **removeSequence** that will remove a contiguous sequence of balls of the same color and of a length equal to or greater than a given value. The sequence must be produced by looking both to the left and to the right of the starting position. The function is shown on the next page.

The function will have one parameter for the index of the initial ball in the sequence, and a second one for the minimum number of balls of the same color that need to compose the sequence. This way we can use it with a parameter of 2 in the situation where a ball was shot onto the stream by the cannon, and with a parameter of 3 for subsequent contiguous sequences created by removing the balls. Basically, we start from the position of the ball to be removed and we check left and right for all the balls of the same color in a contiguous sequence. We use the indexes **first** and **last** for this.

Note that some of the cells in the **ballArray** may be empty because some of the balls could have been removed before, so we have to keep searching when we encounter null elements. Since we can't tell how many active balls we have in between **first** and **last** because of it, we'll also add a counter that is incremented every time we encounter a non-null object. After this, if we have a count of balls at least equal to **min**, then we can remove all the active balls between **first** and **last**. For this, we make them invisible by setting their **state** to a value that doesn't correspond to an existing clip, and then assign to their element of the array **null**. After all this we have to update the values of the **firstMoving**, **lastMoving**, and **ballCount** attributes accordingly.

```
public function removeSequence(b, min)
{
    var first = b-1, last = b+1, count = 1, i;
    while (first >= firstMoving &&
            (!ballArray[first] ||
            ballArray[first].color ==
            ballArray[b].color))
    {
        if (ballArray[first])
        {
            count++;
        }
        first--;
    }
    while (last<ballCount && (!ballArray[last]
            || ballArray[last].color ==
            ballArray[b].color))
    {
        if (ballArray[last])
        {
            count++;
        }
        last++;
    }
    if (count >= min)
    {
        for (i = first+1; i<last; i++)
        {
            if (ballArray[i])
            {
                ballArray[i].setState(4);
                ballArray[i] = null;
            }
        }
        if (lastMoving > first)
        {
            lastMoving = first;
        }
```

```
    if (firstMoving > first)
    {
        firstMoving = last;
        return;
    }
    if (ballCount == last)
    {
        ballCount = lastMoving+1;
        return;
    }
  }
}
```

To test that this function works before using it, we can add the following code in the function **moveStream**, after the call to the function **checkActivate**:

```
if (firstMoving < 20)
{
    removeBall(30);
    moveTimer.stop();
}
```

What we do here is check if a given number of balls have been activated, and call the function on one in particular. We stop the timer to be able to observe the situation. Run the app several times to verify that the function does work as intended. Delete the code afterwards, or comment it out.

Now we can write the function that checks for matching balls on the two sides of the stream that has been removed, pulls the two sides together if they match colors, and deletes the sequence of contiguous color if its length is at least three. Note that this is a recursive process by nature, as the deletion action must restart it. A little planning might be necessary for this one first. If the colors on the two sides match, the sequence on the far side will have to be moved backward progressively in a way that is slow enough for the player to observe it. To achieve this, we need an extra timer in the class. Declare it as a class attribute with the name **backTimer** and initialize it in the constructor.

Let's start with the idea of a single sequence needing to move backward. We'll mark the beginning of the sequence with another class attribute; let's call it **backStart**. Then we need a function that will be attached to **backTimer** as a callback function on a timer event, which can be done in the constructor:

```
backTimer.addEventListener(TimerEvent.TIMER,
                           moveBack);
```

You can see the function **moveBack** on the next page. This function is assuming that the sequence to be moved is adjacent in **ballArray** to the part of the stream that precedes it, but it is not geometrically next to it in the path. This is why we can assume that the ball at index **backStart-1** is not null. If the distance between the ball at index **backStart** and the first one before it is still greater than the ball size, then all the balls that follow **backStart** up to an empty stop or to the end of the stream are moved backward by one point. This movement is applied to their position on the stage and does not affect their index in **ballArray**. Their place in this array does not change during the operation, because this was presumably taken care of by calling the function **shiftSequence** beforehand. If the distance is small enough, then the timer governing the back movement is stopped. For now moment, the function restarts **moveTimer** because we have stopped it in the code above for testing purposes, but once we are passed this stage, that timer doesn't need to be stopped and restarted. At the same time, when the **backTimer** stops, we need to check if another sequence of continuous color of at least 3 balls in length was formed, and proceed to remove it if that is the case. We can accomplish this by calling the function that we have defined before.

```
public function moveBack(event:TimerEvent)
{
    var p1 = ballArray[backStart - 1].spot,
        p2 = ballArray[backStart].spot;
    if (distancePt(p1,p2) > ballSize)
    {
        for (var i=backStart; i<ballCount &&
            ballArray[i]; i++)
        {
            moveBall(ballArray[i], -1);
        }
        p2 = ballArray[backStart].spot;
    }
    else
    {
        backTimer.stop();
        moveTimer.start();
        removeSequence(backStart, 3);
    }
}
```

Note that the function **moveBall** appears to have an extra parameter here. Add a parameter to this function for the speed and give it the default value of 1 (just make the parameter equal to 1). That way the call to this function we had in **moveStream** will still work, but the function can also be used to move a ball by a different amount. We will leave it as an exercise to figure out how to modify that function to take the speed into account.

Now that we have a timer, we have to stop it in the function **removeSequence** in two situations. First, when the condition **firstMoving > first** is true at the end of this function, this means that the sequence that was removed spawned all the way to the area in **ballArray** of balls that haven't been activated and moved to the stage yet. The convention in the game is that a match should not be attempted in that case. So before the **return** statement, add an instruction stopping the **backTimer**. Second, when the condition **ballCount ==** **last** is true, this means that the last sequence of balls that was removed represented the end of the stream. In this case there is also nothing else to connect it to on the far side, and the **backTimer** also needs to be stopped.

We have a little more to go before we can test the functionality. The next step is a function that can be called after the balls in a sequence of continuous color has been removed, tying together the functions **removeSequence** and **moveBack**. This function needs to check if the colors on the two sides of the removed sequence match, and if they do, to shift the continuous sequence on the far side backward in **ballArray** and activate the timer. The function **moveBack** is not directly called as such, but indirectly by activating the timer. This function is shown below.

```
function checkRemoveMatch(first, last)
{
    // check for the sequence being within the
    // active range
    if (first < firstMoving || last >=
                          ballCount)
    {
        backTimer.stop();
        moveTimer.start();
        return;
    }
```

```
    // search for the a non-null ball down from
    // first
    while (first >= firstMoving &&
           !ballArray[first])
    {
        first--;
    }
    // check for a non-null ball up from last
    while (last < ballCount &&
           !ballArray[last])
    {
        last++;
    }
    // if we're out of the active sequence
    // or the colors don't match, nothing to do
    if (first < firstMoving || last >=
        ballCount || ballArray[first].color !=
                     ballArray[last].color)
    {
        return;
    }
    // remove the null balls in between
    shiftSequence(first+1, last);
    // set up to physically move the balls
    // backwards
    backStart = first + 1;
    backTimer.start();
}
```

This function needs to be called with the parameters **first** and **last** as they are in the function **removeSequence**, inside the conditional checking that the **count** is greater than or equal to the parameter **min**, after the 3 conditionals inside checking for special cases. For the testing part, we can add an **else** to the conditional checking the counter and restart the **moveTimer** inside it. This can be removed once the code is properly tested.

At this point you can test the newly added functionality. Everything should be working as expected, except that when the moving stream catches up with the static part of the stream, it doesn't connect with it to restart it, but rather continues on without it. To remedy this, we need to write one more function. In this one we need to start from the index in the **ballArray** following **lastMoving**, and look for the first element that is not null. If we do find one, we need to compare the geometrical position of that ball with the one of the last ball moving. If they happen to be close enough (closer than the ball size), then we need both to shift backwards any balls that are continuously following it in **ballArray**, and to change the value of **lastMoving** to include this part of the stream to the moving interval. Here is this function:

```
function checkMergeStreams()
{
    var i = lastMoving + 1, p1, p2, j;
    while (i<ballCount && !ballArray[i])
    {
        i++;
    }
    if (i < ballCount)
    {
        p1 = ballArray[lastMoving].spot;
        p2 = ballArray[i].spot;
        if (distancePt(p1, p2) <= ballSize)
        {
            shiftSequence(lastMoving+1, i);
        }
    }
}
```

This function must be called from **moveStream** right after the call to **checkActivate**.

Test the functionality that was added several times to make sure that everything works properly, then remove or comment out everything that was used for testing.

Adding a Ball

When the cannon shoots a ball towards the stream, if the color of the ball doesn't match two or more existing balls at the position where the ball crosses the stream, then the ball must be added to the stream instead of causing some of the balls to be removed from it. Let's write a function to handle this situation. We'll assume that we receive as parameter the index of the closest ball in the stream to the one that will be inserted, and the **Ball** object itself. The first thing to determine is the index of the element in the **ballArray** behind which the new ball will be inserted. For this, we'll compare the distance between the ball to be inserted and the balls before and after the closest one in the stream. If the new ball is closer to the ball after the closest one, then the **index+1** is the position before which it should get in. If the new ball is closer to the ball before the closest one, then **index** itself is the place before which the insertion should happen. Figure 24 illustrates this concept.

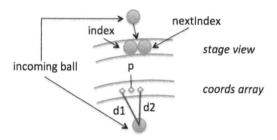

Figure 24. Figuring out where the new ball should be inserted

Two special cases need to be taken into account: if the closest ball is at the beginning or at the end of the stream. If we are at the beginning of the stream, then we need to compare the position of the new ball with the second one on the stream to see if we need to insert it before or after the first ball. A similar argument can be made for the end of the stream.

Once we determine the index of the new ball in **ballArray**, we can use a function called **splice** defined in the **Array** class, that can insert a new element in an array at a given index by shifting all the elements that come after it forward. The second parameter in this function indicates if any elements from the initial array will be deleted. The **ballCount** attribute needs to be incremented in any case, since we've added an element to the array. Both the indexes **firstMoving** and **lastMoving** must also be incremented, but only if they represent indexes larger than the position where we insert the new element.

After we attach the new ball to the stream, we can call the function **removeSequence** with the first parameter being the **index** of the inserted ball, to see if there was a match of at least 3 balls, in which case they can simply be removed. Beforehand we must modify this function **removeSequence** to make it return **true** or **false** to indicate whether a sequence was removed or not. In the conditional "**if (count >= min)**" the function should return **true**, while for all other situations it should return **false**. The second part can be accomplished by adding a single **return false;** statement at the end. The code of the function containing the ideas discussed so far is shown on the next page.

When adding a new ball, if it matches at least two existing balls and the sequence is removed in the function, then there is nothing else to do. Otherwise the balls currently in the stream must be shifted to make place for the new one. The ball to be added to the stream will take the place of the one previously on the index before which it was added. The balls in the sequence after it must be physically shifted forward until the distance between the new ball and the next one is large enough to fit it without overlap. This will require us to add more functionality to handle this situation. It is convenient to add a special function for it.

```
public function addBall(b, index)
{
    var p, d1, d2, p1, nextIndex;
    var bx = b.centerx, by = b.centery;
    p = ballArray[index].spot;

    // calculate the distance d1 to the point
    // before p and d2 to the point after p
    if (p == 0)
    { // first point on the path
        d1 = distance(bx, by, coords[2*p],
                      coords[2*p+1]);
        d2 = distance(bx, by, coords[2*(p+1)],
                      coords[2*p+3]);
    }
    else if (p == pointNum-1)
    { // last point on the path
        d1 = distance(bx, by, coords[2*(p-1)],
                      coords[2*p-1]);
        d2 = distance(bx, by, coords[2*p],
                      coords[2*p+1]);
    }
    else
    {
        d1 = distance(bx, by, coords[2*(p-1)],
                      coords[2*p-1]);
        d2 = distance(bx, by, coords[2*(p+1)],
                      coords[2*p+3]);
    }

    if (d1 < d2)
    { // the point before p was closer
        nextIndex = index;
    }
```

```
else
{ // the point after p was closer
    nextIndex = index+1;
    p = ballArray[index+1].spot;
}

// now add the ball before nextIndex
b.spot = p;
ballArray.splice(nextIndex, 0, b);
ballCount++;
if (lastMoving >= nextIndex)
{
    lastMoving++;
}
if (firstMoving >= nextIndex)
{
    firstMoving++;
}
if (!removeSequence(nextIndex, 3))
{

}
}
```

Let's write a function that makes place for one ball. First, we need to identify the contiguous sequence of balls following the one at the given **index**, that we'll mark by the indexes **first** and **last**. Once this is done, we have to move all the balls between **first** and **last** forward by one point (this involves the **spot** attribute) until the distance between the position of the ball at **index** and the next one in the sequence is at least equal to **ballSize**. Here is this function:

```
public function makeOnePlace(index)
{
    var first = index+1,
        p = ballArray[index].spot,
        last = first;
```

```
if (index == ballCount-1)
{
    return;
}
while (last < ballArray.length &&
       ballArray[last])
{
    last++;
}
var d = distancePt(p,
            ballArray[first].spot);
while (d < ballSize)
{
    for (var i = first; i<last; i++)
    {
        moveBall(ballArray[i]);
    }
    d = distancePt(p,
            ballArray[first].spot);
}
}
```

We can call this function from the empty spot in the last conditional in the function **addBall**. After the empty place was created, we can move the new ball to its correct position:

```
makeOnePlace(nextIndex);
b.move(coords[2*p], coords[2*p+1], p);
```

You can test this function by creating a new ball in the **moveStream** function when some condition becomes true, as for example, **firstMoving < 20**, and then adding it in a given place in the stream, as for example, 10.

The Cannon Class

The last piece of the puzzle is now ready to fall in place. To create this class, first we need to decide on the position and size of the cannon. For this, add the image of the cannon to the stage and manually place it in the right spot and resize it to an acceptable size. Then write down the coordinates and dimensions of the object.

Create a new class called **Cannon**. Copy the function **makeSprite** from the class **Ball**, as well as the import statements that it needs. Add an attribute called **parent** for the stage, matched by a parameter and an initialization in the constructor, as we've done for the class **Ball**. Add attributes for the center **x** and **y** coordinates, like for the class **Ball**, with corresponding parameters in the constructor. Give these parameters in the constructor the default values that you have written down from the stage. Add the attributes **cannonWidth** and **cannonHeight** for the dimensions of this object, and add parameters for them in the constructor with the default values that you wrote down before. Initialize all these attributes properly in the constructor.

The function **makeSprite** needs to be modified to adapt to the fact that the cannon is not a square object. For this, replace the **spriteSize** with two parameters, **spriteW** and **spriteH**, and the **bmpSize** with **bmpW**. We'll assume that we receive the width of the original bitmap and we are resizing the image by the same factor on both sides to preserve the aspect. This is not a mandatory feature, since the scale function applied to the transformation matrix accepts two parameters, but rather a choice made in this case. Add an attribute called **cannonSprite**. Add a function call in the constructor building the bitmap first, call this function to build the sprite, and then add the sprite to the parent.

Going back to the stage, delete the cannon object added by hand and create one using this class instead in the Actions dialog. Copy the function **positionClip** from the class **Ball** and call it from the constructor with **cannonSprite** as parameter. Running the application should now display the cannon in the right place.

Now let's add a function to the class to rotate the cannon. Thinking ahead to the logistics of the operation, the player orients the cannon by moving the mouse, and shoots a ball by clicking on a point on the stage. Thus, we will need to rotate the cannon towards a specific point corresponding to the mouse location. So we'll call this function **rotateToPoint** and it will take two parameters for the position of the point.

First, we'll need to compute the rotation angle that orients the cannon towards the given coordinates. For this, we can compute its tangent by dividing the difference in the **x** coordinate between the position of the cannon and the click point by the difference in the **y** coordinate. Figure 25 illustrates this. Then we can use the function **atan** from the **Math** module returning the angle in radians corresponding to the value of the tangent. This angle is only correct for the angles between $-\pi/2$ to $\pi/2$ (-90 to 90 in degrees); this range represents the two quadrants to the right of the y axis. If the point is in the two quadrants to the left, which is true if the **x** coordinate of the click point is less than the **x** coordinate of the cannon, then we need to add π (180 in degrees) to the value returned by **atan**.

A sprite object in ActionScript has a property called **rotation**, taking a parameter that represent the rotation angle in degrees. This would work perfectly fine for our purpose, except that the rotation is performed around the anchor point of the object, which is the upper left corner by default. Here is a version of the rotation function using this method, in case that works for your program:

```
public function rotateToPoint(px, py)
{
    var angle = 0;
    if (px ! =  centerx)
    {
        // calculate the tangent
        var tan = (py-centery) / (px-centerx);

        // checking the quadrant
        if (px > centerx)
        {
            angle = Math.atan(tan);
        }
        else
        {
            angle = Math.atan(tan) + Math.PI;
        }
    }
    // convert from radians to degrees
    angle = 180*angle/Math.PI;
    cannonSprite.rotation = angle;
}
```

In many cases, though, we would like to rotate the cannon object around a center situated inside the object. If an option of specifying the anchor point explicitly is added to ActionScript, this issue can be solved using that way and the function above does not have to change. In its absence, we can use another feature of sprites, which is a transformation matrix. By declaring a variable of type **Matrix**, we can apply rotations, translations, and scaling operations to it, and then assign this matrix to the sprite object. However, it is not recommended to combine this type of transformation with the rotation defined above.

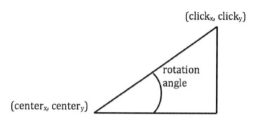

Figure 25. Rotation angle based on the mouse click point

So first, the function call in the constructor positioning the sprite at the coordinates defined by **centerx** and **centery** must be commented out. Moreover, the rotation defined using a transformation matrix uses an angle defined in radians instead of degrees, which means that the instruction in the function **rotateToPoint** converting the angle to degrees must also be commented out. Then, we'll add two attributes to the class, **offsetx** and **offsety**, defining the position of the rotation center inside the cannon object. In the constructor, assign them the values that would work for your object.

Now we're ready to apply the appropriate transformations. We start by translating the object backward by the negative of the values of **offsetx** and **offsety** to move the rotation center to the origin (0, 0). Then we can apply the rotation. Finally, we translate the object back to its original position. These three operations represent the standard procedure for rotations around an arbitrary center. Since we're not setting the **x** and **y** attributes of the sprite directly to place the cannon at its right position on the screen, we need to apply a translation of coordinates **centerx** and **centery** after this. Since the translations can be composed, we can combine the last two translations into a single one. Let us call **rotx** the value **centerx+offsetx**, and **roty** the value **centery+roty**.

These values represent the coordinates of the point around which the cannon is rotated. Let's store them in class variables, as they will be needed again later. Next you can find the code to be added to the function **rotateToPoint**:

```
var transMatrix = new Matrix();
transMatrix.translate(-offsetx, -offsety);
transMatrix.rotate(angle);
transMatrix.translate(rotx, roty);
cannonSprite.transform.matrix = transMatrix;
```

Test this code by adding a call to this function in the constructor with the values 0, 0, and make sure that the cannon is rotated towards the upper left corner of the stage. Test the feature again with each corner of the stage, then comment it out or delete it.

Let's add a **Ball** object to the cannon that can be shot. We can use an actual object of type **Ball** that will be dynamically generated when needed. The color of the object will be generated randomly for every shot. The coordinates of the ball need to start as the position from where it will be shot, and be recomputed when the cannon is rotated.

Declare two attributes in the class Cannon called **shootBall** and **nextBall**, and initialize the first one as an object of the class **Ball** in the constructor. Import the module **Ball** for this purpose.

For the cannon with the shape shown in Figure 19, given that the initial position with an angle of 0 has the cannon perfectly horizontal facing to the right, the ball will be placed at the tip of the cannon shaft. The coordinates of the ball will be given by the following, where **ballRadius** is another class variable with the value equal to **ballSize/2**; the offset of 4 will have to be adjusted to the size of the ball you are using:

```
(centerx + cannonWidth - ballRadius+4,
 centery + offsety - ballRadius)
```

This will make the ball look like it is placed a little less than half way inside the cannon's shaft. The effect is not achieved unless the cannon is displayed in front of the ball. During the execution of the game, the ball will be the last object added as a child to the stage, and thus it will be displayed on top. To place the cannon sprite on top, we can first remove it from the stage by calling a function **removeChild**, and then add it back right away:

```
parent.removeChild(cannonSprite);
parent.addChild(cannonSprite);
```

Now that we have introduced the function **removeChild**, it would be useful to define a function **deleteBall** in the class **Ball** that removes all the sprites from the stage. This way, if the reference in the **Stream** class is also deleted, a garbage collection function can be called to dispose of the object entirely, saving memory for the application. Here is this function, requiring the module **flash.system.System** to be imported first:

```
System.gc();
```

If the cannon is rotated, then this ball will need to be rotated too. We could apply the same kind of rotation to it, but we have to keep in mind that the ball will need to be moved on a straight line towards the click point once released, and then collision detection with the stream will have to be performed. This would be difficult without computing the actual coordinates of the ball. Figure 26 shows what we are trying to accomplish:

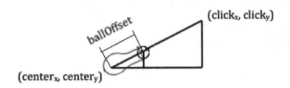

Figure 26. Rotation of the cannon and the ball towards the mouse position

If we denote the difference between the rotation center of the cannon and the center of the ball by **ballOffset**, its value is determined by the initial placement of the ball:

```
ballOffset = cannonWidth + 4 - offsetx;
```

This can be declared as a class attribute and initialized in the constructor. Then in the **rotation** function we can use the fact that the proportions between the different sides of the small triangle in this figure are equal to the proportions between the corresponding sides in the big one. If we denote by **(bx, by)** the position of the center of the ball relative to the rotation center, and by **d** the distance between the click point and the rotation center, then they can be computed as

```
d = distance(rotx, roty, px, py);
bx = (px - rotx) * ballOffset / d;
by = (py - roty) * ballOffset / d;
```

By adding these to the rotation center, we obtain the position of the center of the ball. If we place the ball at these coordinates right away, it will appear that the top left corner of the ball is always placed right in the middle of the cannon at every angle, because that is the anchor point for the sprite. If we want the center of the ball to be placed at this position instead, we have to subtract the ball radius from each coordinate.

We can put all of these ideas together in a function called `rotateBallToPoint`:

```
public function rotateBall(px, py)
{
    var d = distance(rotx, roty, px, py);
    var bx = (px - rotx) * ballOffset / d;
    var by = (py - roty) * ballOffset / d;
    shootBall.move(rotx+bx-ballRadius,
                   roty+by-ballRadius, -1);
}
```

This may already be enough to place the ball in the right place for every angle. If there is enough of a difference between the radius of the ball and the width of the cannon mouth, and the ball does not appear centered, you may need to move it on a line perpendicular to the rotation direction (or a line from the rotation center towards the click point). Let's denote by "**adjust**" the length of the estimated necessary adjustment. We need to project it on the line on which we need to move the ball. The perpendicular to a vector **(vx, vy)** is obtained as either **(-vy, vx)** or **(vy, -vx)**. Thus, the adjustment can be achieved by the computing the following values:

```
var cx = -( py - roty) * adjust / d;
var cy = (px - rotx) * adjust / d;
```

and then adding them to or subtracting them from the coordinates of the ball. Try both versions and keep the one that works.

Mouse Event

For an easier test of the **rotation** function, we now would be a good time to get the cannon to follow the mouse on the screen and rotate in its direction. For this, we first need to add a function that can be called in the event of the mouse moving. This function is finding the coordinates of the mouse pointer form attributes of the event itself, and then calling the functions we have written before to accomplish the action.

```
public function rotateEvent(eve:MouseEvent)
{
    var mousex = eve.stageX;
    var mousey = eve.stageY;
    rotateToPoint(mousex, mousey);
    rotateBall(mousex, mousey);
}
```

Then we need to add an event listener to cause this function to be called. Since this event is not related to any specific object on the screen in terms of the mouse position, we can add the event directly to the stage, stored as the class variable **parent**. The following code must be added to the constructor:

```
parent.addEventListener(MouseEvent.MOUSE_MOVE,
                        rotateEvent);
```

Test this new functionality to see if the rotation performs as expected. Note that this is an event that happens when the mouse is simply moved on the screen.

Shooting the Ball

The application is ready now to add the functionality of clicking the mouse to shoot the ball. We'll need a new function that will later be linked to a mouse click event.

To shoot the ball, we'll need to set the speed of the ball. Let's first declare a class variable called **ballSpeed** and initialize it with some value in the constructor, as for example, 5. This will represent the distance that the ball travels in each iteration. Let's add two more variables called **ballSpeedX**, **ballSpeedY**, that will represent the projection on x and y of this speed considered in the direction of the current rotation. We will also need a timer to animate the ball that can be started in the mouse click function. Let's call this the **ballTimer**; add it as a class variable and initialize it in the constructor as:

```
ballTimer = new Timer(50);
ballTimer.addEventListener(TimerEvent.TIMER,
                            moveBall);
```

The function **moveBall** still needs to be defined.

We will start by writing the function to be linked to the mouse click. The function needs to compute the speed of the ball first, and then start the timer. The ball was already placed in the right position by the function **rotateEvent**. To compute the projection of the speed along x and y we use the same idea used to place the ball in the right position.

```
public function clickEvent(eve:MouseEvent)
{
    var px = eve.stageX;
    var py = eve.stageY;
    var d = distance(rotx, roty, px, py);

    ballSpeedX = (px - rotx) * ballSpeed / d;
    ballSpeedY = (py - roty) * ballSpeed / d;
    ballTimer.start();
}
```

Now let's link this with the mouse click event in the constructor:

```
parent.addEventListener(MouseEvent.MOUSE_UP,
                        clickEvent);
```

The **MOUSE_UP** event is generated when the mouse button is released.

To move the ball, it may be convenient to add the following function to the class **Ball** first:

```
public function moveBy(px, py)
{
    move(centerx+px, centery+py, spot);
}
```

Then we can call it from the function linked to the timer in the class **Cannon**.

```
public function moveBall(event:TimerEvent)
{
    shootBall.moveBy(ballSpeedX, ballSpeedY);
}
```

The game should be working with the new functions, but the ball does not stop when it gets off the screen. For this, we can add a function to the **Ball** class checking if its coordinates are still on the stage or not. We have to take into account that the anchor point of the ball is in the top left corner. Thus, for the bottom and right borders of the stage, we can just compare the coordinates of the object with the dimensions of the stage. For the top and left borders, the anchor point could be outside the stage, but part of the ball might still be visible. The anchor point is out of the stage on the left or the top when one of its coordinates is negative. To make sure the entire ball is not visible anymore, we need to check that the anchor point is beyond the border by a whole size of the ball. This means that one of its coordinates must be less than the negative of the size of the ball. The function checking for all of these cases can be seen below.

```
public function isOnStage()
{
    if (centerx < -size || centery < -size)
    {
        return false;
    }
    else if (centerx > parent.stageWidth ||
                centery > parent.stageHeight)
    {
        return false;
    }
    return true;
}
```

Now going back to the **moveBall** function in the class **Cannon**, we can check if the ball is out of the stage and stop the timer if that is the case.

```
if (!shootBall.isOnStage())
{
    ballTimer.stop();
}
```

One last thing that we can do before starting to work on the collision detection is to prevent the function rotating the cannon from interfering with the function moving the ball once it has left the cannon. For this, in the rotating function we can test if the ball timer is currently active, and if it is, we can skip the function call that rotates the ball. The **Timer** class in ActionScript 3 has an attribute called "**running**" that can be used for this purpose. Go back to the function **rotateEvent** and add the following conditional before the function call rotating the ball, then close the brace after the call:

```
if (!ballTimer.running)
{
```

A similar issue appears in the function **clickEvent**: if we click again while a ball is currently running, it starts going in a different direction. So add the same conditional to the function **clickEvent**, and place the entire body of the function inside it.

After the ball currently in motion has reached its destination or gone out of the screen, we can bring the next one in by moving the mouse again, but it would be preferable if it appeared without having to do it. This can be achieved by adding a call to the function **rotateBall** in the function **moveBall** right after stopping the timer. This requires though the current position of the mouse on screen. The **stage** object, referenced in the **Cannon** class as the **parent**, stores this position in the attributes **mouseX** and **mouseY**. Then they can be used after the timer is stopped to rotate the ball:

```
rotateBall(parent.mouseX, parent.mouseY);
```

Collision Detection

The next stage in the operation is the collision detection between the moving ball and the stream. This operation is more easily implemented in the **Stream** class.

The collision detection function will have to go through the entire stream of active balls and compute the distance between the position of the moving ball and the position of the balls in the stream. If any of the latter is at a distance less than the size of the ball to the former, then we have collision.

There are some precautions that need to be taken, though. If the ball moves at too great a speed, it might skip the stream in one step, as illustrated in Figure 27. To avoid this, one can use a smaller speed and decrease the delay in the `ballTimer` instead. If the ball's movement is still too slow, one can have a collision detection speed of a value equal to the stage screen divided by a factor, for example, 5. The position of the ball could change 5 times using the small increment, and the collision detected for each step. Then the actual sprite would only be moved on the stage in the 5th step.

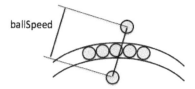

Figure 27. The shooting ball could miss the intersection with the stream

To implement this feature, let's add a class variable in the class **Cannon** called **collisionSteps** and assign it a value in the constructor, as for example, 5. You may have to decrease the value of **ballSpeed**. This will represent the number of steps that the ball will be moved by for the purposes of the collision detection before the position of the object on the stage is actually updated. Figure 28 illustrates this concept, where the transparent circles represent positions of the ball computed for the collision detection, while the dark ones are actually displayed on the stage.

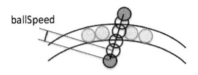

ballSpeed

Figure 28. The collision intersection steps

Let's assume that we'll write a function in the **Stream** class called **detectCollision** taking the position of the ball as parameters and returning either -1 if we have no collision, or the index in the stream array of the closest ball if there is a collision. We still need a reference to the stream in the class **Cannon**. Let's add a parameter to the constructor, called **theStream**, and a class variable called **mainStream**, and assign to it the value of **theStream** in the constructor. For the last step, go to the Actions window while selecting the .**fla** project itself, in Frame 1, and add the variable storing the stream as a second parameter in the function call creating the cannon.

We'll also use the function **addBall** that we defined earlier in the class **Stream**. This function requires one parameter for the ball to be added, and the index in the array where it fits best. Then let's change the **move** function to implement the collision steps, as shown on the next page.

In this function we check for every collision step whether we have a collision with the stream or not. If we do have a collision, we use the index returned by the collision detection function to add the ball that was shot to the stream. Since at this point the **Stream** class takes over the behavior of the ball, we don't need a reference to it in the **Cannon** class. Thus, we can make the variable that was storing this reference **null**. Note that this will not delete the ball object, but only remove its reference from the Cannon class. We must take care to also terminate the `for` loop if this happens. Then after the loop, if the **shootBall** reference is still in the class **Cannon**, meaning that the ball did not collide with the stream yet, then we move it to its current position, which will also update the sprite on the stage. Otherwise we generate a new ball and place it at a position outside the stage. This way it will be properly rotated in place in the next conditional and also cause the ball-moving timer to stop.

```
public function moveBall(event:TimerEvent)
{
    var bx = shootBall.centerx,
        by = shootBall.centery, index;
    for (var i = 0; i<collisionSteps &&
                    shootBall; i++)
    {
        bx +=  ballSpeedX;
        by +=  ballSpeedY;
        index = mainStream.detectCollision(bx,
                                    by);
        if (index ! =  -1)
        {
            shootBall.move(bx, by, -1);
            mainStream.addBall(shootBall,
                            index);
            shootBall = null;
        }
    }
    if (!shootBall)
    {
        shootBall = new Ball(parent,
            -ballSize-1, -ballSize-1, 0,
            ballSize);
    }
    else
    {
        shootBall.move(bx, by, -1);
    }
}
```

```
if (! shootBall.isOnStage())
{
    ballTimer.stop();
    rotateBall(parent.mouseX,
               parent.mouseY);
}
}
```

Now let's add the collision detection function in the class **Stream**. In this function we want not only to find a ball in the stream that presents a collision with the shot ball, but we want to return the index of the closest ball in the stream to the one that was shot. For this, we'll assume that the balls that collide with the ball are in a contiguous sequence. Thus, we scan the stream while we haven't found a collision or until the end of the array. For every position in the ball array that is not empty, we store the distance between the position of the ball and the point **(bx, by)** in the variable **d**. This way we can check if this distance is less than or equal to the diameter of the ball. We'll also store the minimum such distance over the stream array in the variable **mind** and the **index** where it was found. The **index** is initialized as -1 because that is not a valid subscript in the array. A situation where **index** is not -1 anymore and **d** has become greater than the ball size means that we have now passed the set of balls that are in collision with the one being shot, and we can stop checking further.

For paths that may be recoiling on themselves where there might be multiple points of collision with the ball, one can simply remove the first part of the continuation condition in this function altogether, and keep it as

while (i < ballArray.length)

```
public function detectCollision(bx, by)
{
    var index = -1, i = 0, mind = ballSize+1,
        d = 0;
    while ((index < 0 || d <= ballSize) &&
            i < ballArray.length)
    {
        if (ballArray[i])
        {
            d = distance(bx, by,
                        ballArray[i].centerx,
                        ballArray[i].centery);
            if (d <= ballSize)
            {
                if (d < mind)
                {
                    mind = d;
                    index = i;
                }
            }
        }
        i++;
    }
    return index;
}
```

On Your Own

Once the program has reached this point and is working, the
following functionality can be added:

- The power-up feature of slowing the stream's movement,
  pushing the stream back, or exploding, generated randomly.
- A score.
- Checking if the stream is empty to declare the game (or
  level) won; checking if the stream has reached the end of
  the path to declare the game (or life) lost.
- Checking for the colors still present in the stream and only
  generating new balls to be shot in those colors. This can be
  accomplished by having a counter for the number of balls in
  the stream in each color. A small array can keep track of the

colors with counters that have not yet reached 0. A random number can be used to choose a color form that array. Once a counter reaches 0, its color is removed from the array of colors.

Final Note

We hope that the tutorials and explanations will be enough to get the reader started on his or her quest to become a proficient game programmer. We wish you good luck on your journey.

References

Adobe Inc. (2013): Adobe ActionScript ® 3.0 (AS3) API Reference. Web site, http://help.adobe.com/en_US/FlashPlatform/reference/actionscript/3/index.html

M. Collins (2001): *Linux game programming*, Prima Tech.

J. H. Conway (2000): *On Numbers and Games*, 2nd edition, A. K. Peters, Wellesley, Massachusetts.

J. D. Funge (2004): *AI for Games and Animation*, A. K. Peters, Natick, Massachusetts.

J. R. Hall, Loki Software (2001): *Programming Linux Games*, Loki Software Inc., No Starch.

A. Kirmse (2004): *Game Programming Gems 4*, Charles River Media.

G. Maestri (1999): *Digital Character Animation 2*, New Riders.

M. Morrison (2004): *Beginning Game Programming*, Sams.

K. Salen, E. Zimmerman (2004): *Rules of Play: Game Design Fundamentals*, MPIT Press.

B. Suits (2005): Games, Life, and Utopia, Broadview Press.

ABOUT THE AUTHOR

Dana Vrajitoru is an associate professor at Indiana University South Bend where she teaches games programming, artificial intelligence, computer graphics, and more.

www.ingramcontent.com/pod-product-compliance
Lightning Source LLC
Chambersburg PA
CBHW051235050326
40689CB00007B/925